LIFE EXPECTANCY

PRAISE FOR *LIFE EXPECTANCY*

* * *

"These are poems that live 'between grief and happiness'—poems about struggle, hope, acceptance, anger, poems full of things that matter, and contradiction, poems extraordinary for their compassion and tenderness even in witness of terrible happenings. And, above all, poems of great beauty, spoken in a sure and grace-filled voice."

—MOLLY GLOSS, author of *The Hearts of Horses* and *The Jump-Off Creek*

* * *

"Kirsten Rian's grasp of the universe is unique and enormous. She can lead the reader's vision, in the space of two lines, from 'the velocity of sky' to 'the distance/between you and me.' There are hard subjects in these pages: a CT scan or a tumor inside a child's skull; yet the poetry is lovely no matter what, since her language remains luminous and musical.

Her poems are like the trees she describes in the poem, 'Indivisible': 'Sometimes on windy days I watch trees. And the strongest branches always sway the farthest, batting about the air, holding on to nothing and everything at the same time.' The scope of this work—both geographical and emotional—is huge. It holds on to nothing as it lets go and allows the rhythms of language to hold it aloft; and it holds on to everything as it tackles even the hardest of subjects, with an almost Plathian sensitivity to the consonants and vowels within each word."

—JUDITH BARRINGTON, prize-winning poet and memoirist, author of *Lifesaving; A Memoir* (winner of the Lambda Book Award and runner up for the PEN/Martha Albrand Award for the memoir) and the best selling *Writing the Memoir: From Truth to Art*. Among other awards for her poetry is the Gregory O'Donoghue International Poetry Prize

* * *

"Kirsten Rian's *Life Expectancy* comes forth in three parts because her poems embrace questions of abused life and vital hope from myriad directions. These poems demand an unblinking stare at cruelty, and offer intimate consolation in moments of grace, sending a small torch for survival in dark caves of human trouble. Rian knows the terrors of war in a distant land that can splash the news, and the often hidden terrors of local life, both can hurt at the bone in equal measure. Pain is certain, she says, but the reasons are more complicated—and this is what requires the intricate delivery of her poems. 'Between grief and happiness,' these dense blessings bud from her struggle, and will blossom in you."

—Kim Stafford, author of *100 Tricks Every Boy Can Do: How My Brother Disappeared*

LIFE EXPECTANCY

poetry by
KIRSTEN RIAN

redbat books
La Grande, Oregon
2018

Thanks to the editors of the following journals and anthologies where some of the poems first found a home: *Berberis Press/Lewis & Clark College, Broadriver Review, Daylight Books, Exterminating Angel Press, HatjeCantz Publishing, Haven Press, Jefferson Quarterly, On the Issues Magazine, Ooligan Press, Oregonian, Portland Magazine, Rhino,* and *Upstreet.*

© 2018 by Kirsten Rian.

All rights reserved.

This book or any portion thereof may not be reproduced or used in any manner whatsoever without the express written permission of the publisher except for the use of brief quotations in a book review.

Printed in the United States of America

First Edition: April 3, 2018

Trade Paperback ISBN: 978-1-946970-97-8

Library of Congress Control Number: 2018937159

Published by
redbat books
2901 Gekeler Lane
La Grande, OR 97850
www.redbatbooks.com

Text set in Baskerville

Cover art:
"What Remains," watercolor by Kirsten Rian

Book design by
Kristin Summers, redbat design | www.redbatdesign.com

TABLE OF CONTENTS

I. *Migration* 9
    Embedment 11
    Migration 12
    Time Before Birds 13
    Apostrophe 17
    Mime Logic 18
    In the Last Dream the Map was Cut in Quarters
        and Taped to the Window Panes 19
    Night Landing 20
    The Widow Who Wasn't 21
    If a straight line 23
    First Sight 25
    New Day Rising 26
    I remember now, the end of the world 27
    Distinctive Wound Characteristics 28
    CT: a spiral scanner rotates around an axis 29
    When Audrey Hepburn Sings *Moon River* 30
    While Braiding My Daughter's Hair 33
    Growth, I 34
    Growth, II 35
    Growth, III 36
    Life Expectancy, I 37
    Life Expectancy, II 38
    Life Expectancy, III 39
    Life Expectancy, IV 40
    Soup 41
    Flight Patterns 42
    Red 44
    From up here 45
    "It's better to know in advance that we are going to fail." 47
    Small Craft Through Foreign Skies 48
    Indivisible 50
    Apples of Silk Road 52
    Pieces 54
    Border Crossing 55
    Home 56
    Treaty 57
    Adjacent 59

"You, however, had taken off in the hope of finding a rift in the sky." 60
Invention 61
Fugue 62
Glacier Dust Makes Apple Grafts Grow 65
Entomology 67
Boden Catalogue 68
An opeidoscope illustrates sound with rays of light, ... 70
Blink 72

II. *And Other Sounds* 75
Radiation 77
Ramps 81
An opeideoscope illustrates sound with rays of light, II .. 84
Soundtrack 87
Mapmaking 90
Fight for Your Right 93
The Night Stevie Ray Died 97
What Happiness Looks Like 101
Inverse Correlation 104

III. *What Remains* 107
Sitting In a Hut with a Rimur Chanter 109
Vibrato 111
Migration, II 112
Migration, III 113
The Waltz of Siglufjörður 114
Glossary 115
Eyes Like Mine 117
Keeper of Bells 118
Rock-Paper-Scissors 119
Monologue, I 120
Monologue, II 121
Monologue, III 122
Apostrophe 124
Statistics 126
Lumpfish 127
Ancestry 129

About the Author 133

To Sophia-Marie and Clarke
for everything

* * *

And to my mother and grandmother,
who mothered through their own trauma the best they could

I.
Migration

EMBEDMENT

I'm up there talking about war, the kind with Kalashnikovs and scuds

At the Q & A someone asks if I've changed

My hand tucks my errant hair behind my ear

And in that scurrying second

My mother's hand is gathering my hair off my neck

I am in my yellow kitchen baking chocolate cake

I am clipping my son's nails, his round soft perfect toes

I am sitting in the courtyard at Stanford Medical Center waiting
    for the next operating room call from the surgeon
    or anesthesiologist. I am watching people with tubes
    and bags and silver rolling contraptions shuffle past.
    For hours I study flowers.
    "Your boy's still doing just fine,"
    they say each time they call

I am home walking the dog, and it is not raining, and there are sparrows

My daughter calls from the tub, asking me to show her how to shave

I am putting on Sarah Vaughan because it reminds me of my mother

My thoughts skid and I am back in front of 200 people

Asking how I've changed

I will tell you:

I have realized there are places on this earth I will never see

The streetlight in front of my house is a shard of sun at 3 am reminding
    me to pray

Somewhere between grief and happiness is my life

MIGRATION

Suppose, then, all the birds in the world line up
and perch along the equator—for luck, for love.
It is spring and migrating patterns confluence
back and forth—give me what I need in the guise
of what I want, call it north, south, be it marriage,
divorce. Yesterday while walking the dog my boy
tells me he still cries alone in his room a lot.
Suppose, then, we wake from hibernation—
for light, for longer days. It is spring and my daughter
mows the lawn with our hand pusher. Later,
she yells at me, I tell her to clean up her mouth,
she emerges from her room 30 minutes later
with *silence is everything* scrawled up and down
and around her right arm, she walks around the house
with her arm held up like a banner, like a drawn sword,
like an estuary jutting off from the river toward some ocean
I can hear but can't see. But it's there,
covering seventy-one percent of my earth, it's there
pounding my shore, the one she's headed for
while I wait here for the coroner's report that will arrive
in week eight and now in week six I'm thinking no one
dies of nothing, no one walks into a hospital and
dies of nothing, do they? Suppose, then, all the birds
of the world line on the wire strung in front of our house
like a forecast, like a sign, like a treaty delivered on wings
through air in place of your apology for leaving us here.

TIME BEFORE BIRDS

Hammering

into the

sound

—

Do not point out

what's left—it is not

conditional, something lost,

something

remains

—

No

—

I wrote

your obituary

sitting at your desk,

it was late,

about 11:30,

the outline, the

bullet points

of a man's life.

The newspaper

has a word limit.

I was never good

at editing.

I mean

everything I say

—

I am against

forgetting

—

Stone by stone by stone

—

But, no,

the beginning *before* the beginning,

our son asks,

spooning cereal

into his mouth

—

A year on Mars is 687 days

So there, we'd be half our age

—

Start all over again all over again all over again

—

It's not

a revolution

to chase

the familiar

when memory

is all

I've got

—

Big bang

—

Mama, he insists,

who started

the beginning-beginning

—

Well, I don't know

—

That's what I've got:

'I don't know'

—

and stones,

a handful

in my pocket

to drop

from a suspension bridge

in the woods

and call

it love

APOSTROPHE

The first word spoken on the moon was okay

I've begun quoting you, that's the language—now

The first telegraph message tapped by Samuel Morse,
    what hath God wrought?

The first words spoken over the telephone by Alexander Bell,
    Watson, please come here. I want you

The first words spoken by Thomas Edison over the phonograph,
    Mary had a little lamb

Air where the music hangs

Feast on in-between

Theology of lace is in the spaces

And this is how we speak—now

I need to gather my things. I am gathering my—

Recalcitrant dogwood blossoms

Did I tell you it's already April? The only euphony is after-thought

By the way, last week our daughter got her period for the first time.
And yesterday I leaned over in the car to kiss her goodbye. She bobbed
her head like a sand swallow and kissed the air around my cheek
so not to smear her lip gloss. I reached for her hand, she hovered hers
atop my palm so not to mess the nail polish she had just applied
sitting in the passenger seat while I drove her to school

It was all air. It's always all air
The kind to fly through
To get somewhere
    Somewhere warm

MIME LOGIC

I realize the space you inhabited before you died doesn't get filled—

it remains a boxspring
my son jumps on
because he still believes
he might maybe touch the ceiling.

Marriage, answers, that I sleep better alone—I used to believe in
    some things

Ours was transparent
and maybe that's why
I like waking early.
The light is like prayer,

not fully realized, so when I sit at the table with coffee I am without
    expectation

and might possibly reach up
again for the string
that dangles from the light
like an apology.

IN THE LAST DREAM
THE MAP WAS CUT IN QUARTERS
AND TAPED TO THE WINDOW PANES

The worst part about insomnia
is you stop dreaming
because you never leave earth.

The worst part about making a plan
is believing in it:

divorce, the mass in your kid's head, snow.

Once we kept a snowball,
in our freezer for six months.
It was dirty and named Harold.
At first I protested, but my kid
insisted, said he needed to remember
the day it snowed.

The worst part about memory
is it cannot be forgotten,
the plans part,
the everything switchbacking
down the mountain part.

NIGHT LANDING

"I am giving up the landmarks by which I might be taking my bearings."
—*Antoine de Saint-Exupéry*, pilot

The hours that counted were measured by how much sand

was left in my pocket after charming you on the beach,
by the derivative of a voice over the single engine

as I remembered
back that far. You know,
time is not what I wanted—
fly past the horizon enough
and the moon on the starboard side
cuts visibility in half every time.

Besides, it's change in atmospheric pressure
that's going to get us all in the end, anyway.

No, when hovering
over the Sargasso Sea
at night looking for landmarks,
it was etymology I wanted,

anthropological evidence it's not words that remain,
it's the space left when it quiets, the assumption of miracles.

And now it is morning
even thought it is still dark,
it is morning—not last night, not last year,
it is morning.

On this earth it is always morning, somewhere.

THE WIDOW WHO WASN'T

A half truth: I wanted to trust the social worker who knelt
and looked in our kids' eyes: "Your dad is not going to look the same,"
then stood and guided us through the crowded ER to the room
down the hall. I wanted to believe your appearance was all we had
to worry about. Let me try this again: I'll play the social worker:
Your dad is not going to look the same because he is dead.

But he left off that last part and when we got to the room you actually
did look the same. You looked like you look when you nap at Neskowin,
or fall asleep watching Michigan on Saturdays. And your wife
who was not your wife but who was your wife and your son
and your daughter, we just stood there looking at you, I think trying
to find the way you didn't look the same, like the man said.

It must have been loud in there, I mean, ERs are loud places
with machines beeping and people talking and shoe heels clicking
on linoleum. There's a pace to the sounds, too, quick and in motion
the doctors and nurses moving, patients and their people sick or in pain
or messed up and all those things ricochet sound against
the acoustical tiles. But all I remember from that night is white noise
buffering like a wind tunnel, and air thick enough to hold us all up,
and two nurses and two doctors staring at us and no one saying
anything, just the heavy blurring whoosh. NASA researchers
use wind tunnels to study how aircrafts fly. Some are just
several inches square, others test full-size planes. Some wind tunnels
function at hypersonic speed, testing what can withstand
over 4,000 miles per hour of life passing by. I don't need that.
That already happened. A chime would be nice. From somewhere,
faintly at first, then continuing at regular intervals, gradually gaining
resonance and tone, voluminously filling every corner.

A full truth: I get annoyed when other people get food trains or flowers
or crowd-funding campaigns. At least I recognize this is not
an admirable response. It's January. The month of fables. Years after.
We are supposed to be fine by now, we were supposed to be fine
when it happened: The kids are already living with you, they said.

In some ways maybe easier, they said. We learned to tune it out,
saving birdsong for when it got bad, modulating absence
by talking to you in the park up on Alameda. Here, lean close, listen:

it is still like wildflowers here.

IF A STRAIGHT LINE

If the note of a birdsong filled air from the tree to the sky
in a straight line, we could follow the song

and hear silence on one side, and music on the other,
and the clarity of a clear sound like clear water

would orient through to the other side of everything
that ever mattered, that ever could, sonically illuminating

what we are supposed to have figured out by now.

But of course, a birdcall uncoils and releases itself
across air like fog through trees, forcing forgiveness

of the windstream for pushing notes and nuance
in every direction, while the river below,

flowing under the sound, courses forward, ever forward,
the fluency of gravity and determination of current

to move around and over and despite rocks, fallen branches.

It is not terra firma wisdom, this easy and inevitable flow,
this kind of trust, and neither is music from birds, for that matter.

Or the winter light splaying the gray long days, or prayer
or memory. Yet here I stand on the banks of this river,

needing every single thing I cannot see and do not understand,
watching the water and shadows of trees synchronously

move together, carrying everything in their path toward somewhere.

And where does happiness fit into all this—what's the sound
of hope and belief and of finally just letting go?

And where the river melts into some ocean
is that the inevitable blending of intention and outcome,

rimmed by a never-shifting horizon line splitting sky and earth?
Or, rather, wrapping around like string or arms

holding the world, its sounds, our mistakes, the proof together.

FIRST SIGHT

I translate to: disbelief of sun
a smooth, flat place: wrinkled with shadow

a stone's throw: up to the pocket of the sky
except linen clouds break: the silence

and that place: where you land
dropped there: in front of me,

I cannot move: because you
are blocking: my path

it is all right: you're the garnet
reflecting light: I didn't know I didn't see

and everyone is broken: everyone misses someone
and every morning: waking up hurts a little bit

and the sun, its target: the dark
and the line between us: equator, horizon, string

NEW DAY RISING

—Hüsker Dü

Since it's today, we start
all over again expanding some
long-imagined plan to get there,
step by step, now by now. And
if the ivory morning sky between
6:30 and 7 is the truth of the matter,
then the unfolding begins here–
nothing is banished, forgotten,
or even forgiven, because it's
past the need for that now,
the influence of the living exported
to somewhere else, where all the
almost saids, came close to doings,
and might haves reconcile and give in
to the relief of loving. Just loving.

I REMEMBER NOW,
THE END OF THE WORLD

      What difference could it possibly make
whether fennel or cilantro, whether the beet is chopped coarsely
or sliced thinly, though in that case,
      when held up to the light, is like skin, and I like

making something out of nothing, even if
it is dripping red across the white porcelain sink

It is blood spots in snow from where the bb grazed the wing
of the quail—
      —still out there somewhere. I wanted to save it but he
started the truck, mom was waiting

Thousands of days have passed since then

      What difference has that actually made

I remember now, yesterday, I tried to save you—
      your ear drains yellow like a pin-pricked sun

DISTINCTIVE WOUND CHARACTERISTICS

The Stanford surgeon gives me a photo he took
after they'd cut into my boy's head, before
they took what parts of the pearlescent orb—
nestled in red, stuck in the bones—
they could.

A forensic scientist is lecturing on distinctive
wound characteristics. She projects images
of a skull. A bullet enters and makes one precise hole.
Cracks run off like atlas riverlines.
On the other side, however, the bone is blown out.
"There is more damage upon exit," she says.

One day in early 2000 our son's replicating cells
were told, *build this build this*. And his body did.
There is no exit wound on his head.

Bullet and bone fragments can be tightly patterned
to give the story of the gun, or
of the hand that held the gun.

When I was pregnant I kept a journal, in it I wondered
the color of his eyes. Even
his daily pain is a perfect pattern I: cannot break.

If a life past this one, I'd return as a forensic astronomer—
    there is such a field.

CT: A SPIRAL SCANNER ROTATES AROUND AN AXIS

I whip egg whites because you asked for meringues
    and today, there is nothing to hit.

So, I loop my hand and thread plausible, invisible circles,
    my wrist aches, liquid sets
    into mountain peaks.

Like this. Like this cycle of day, the refined declivity of dawn.

Like the heads on top of the stick figures you used to draw.

I'm still here because kindness, primitive. Hope, violent.
    And compassion, compassion is desperate
    and impenetrable like the jar of cinnamon
    I accidentally knocked off the counter,
    sending plumes slowly drifting to the floor,
    settling evenly, quietly, completely
    across the hardwoods,

for you to step in when you enter the kitchen, leaving a path
    of footprints and evidence
    you were here.

WHEN AUDREY HEPBURN SINGS *MOON RIVER*

I.

To thin the dense trees
of our history
I must gather
all the broken branches
cracked by heavy winter
rain and wind,
blown and settled
along with pine needles and leaves
to the forest floor,
clear them out of the way.
Then fell the trees
left standing.

II.

What I miss
collects on the back porch,
the summer sandal,
the trowel, you.

III.

The facial nerve runs behind the tumor, now this is a fact.
"In my hands, the risks are negligible," the surgeon says,
jotting something on his pad.
They wheel my boy
down the white, shiny-floored hall
in the shiny chrome bed. Will he still
have a smile when he wakes up?

IV.

The swiss chard survived
the winter. He rips off a leaf
and tears pieces into bites
before turning the scooter around,
back down the sidewalk.

V.

Birds land on wires,
painters paint fruit,
windows open
and breath of the world
pushes past the stale
air of routine and closed doors,
and of all I forget to say,
stitching a line in the air
when he asks, over
and over and over
if he's going to be
all right, if his head
will ever stop hurting.

VI.

I've learned not to trust,
criss-crossing roads
leading to places
I'm sure I've been
or would like to visit,
or forget, or just drive
past, eyes straight ahead,
window down.

VII.

With blue sidewalk chalk
he draws a train track
running the entire length
of the block, then
he runs up and down,
and up and down,
a needle threading
every single thing
I could lose.

WHILE BRAIDING MY DAUGHTER'S HAIR

I count years
like counting after thunder claps,

waiting for lightning
to scar the sky.

You collect erasers,
unzip the quiet with

your katydid humming,
the din of wings rubbing

back and forth against boredom.
You have waited in waiting rooms,

and for that I am sorry.
You have stared out windows

and counted cars.
One day you gave me

your wooden doll,
the one with the red yarn hair.

My talk-to doll, you said.
I am to tell it everything.

My words are blades
of grass holding

the outline of our bodies,
from where we lay

watching the sky,
waiting for rain.

GROWTH, I

My son's mastoid tumor was the size of an almond

Mine, a walnut. The new one in my parotid gland, a pine nut

The three in my abdomen, a pea, a cashew, and kumquat

> Each English Ivy berry holds up to five seeds birds disperse

> The vines climb and snake along, filling any open speck of space, its rootlets and stems clinging to walls, tree trunks. It can fell a tree from its weight of vine upon vine upon vine

History rewrites itself with each invasion

Happily? The covenant of the clear-minded

Do not speak to me of habitat, home
    —hiding inside a closet, a body, a garden

I feel its shape in me

GROWTH, II

To you, who listens to the near misses,
notices how you see and then pays attention
to how you remember what you see:

Legacy, I commend you, inhabiting me
without my consent. It's no different
from allegiance too long to Himalayan Blackberry

because I like the sound of the name,
because its vines are at this point too threaded
into my garden boxes, against my backyard fence—

I'm simply tired and this is not who I used to be.
'Daughter plants form where canes touch ground.'
'Remove root crown,' this is what the experts said,

the exact words they used. Accuse the royal truth
of my genealogy with tumors growing
where they needn't—I just want to love what's left.

GROWTH, III

Near Belgrade, excavated burial sites
revealed symbols of an undecipherable language,
Vinča, dating back to 5th millennium BC
believed by some to be the oldest
form of writing ever found

Tectonic shifts are circumstantial,
mountain ranges link, pull apart
and thousands of years later I'm standing here
wondering if it was worth the wait,
this talk of things we don't understand

Vinča is also *periwinkle*, invasive ground cover
my mother taught me to thin, fingers in the soil,
pull at the roots, or was it close the door,
stand close to me—which is it going to be?
I need to know if duplicities of language

translate on medical reports, in history books

LIFE EXPECTANCY, I

I ask her, is it easy to catch a cab from here?

Midnight. Berlin. Train platform.

Take the S-Bahn with me, I'll show you, she says.

Barbara is 70, a filmmaker, retelling the story
of a Jewish girl killed by Nazis. She places
cut-outs from blown up photos in the exact locations
where the family lived. The girl's sister
is still alive in Poland and tells stories as the soundtrack.

The train stops, we hurriedly exchange cards.

Snow. Streetlights. The ring of the pension bell into the quiet.

Concentric circles of memory, cell memory.

LIFE EXPECTANCY, II

Menshay from Delhi is traveling to Portland
to meet her husband. They have been apart
for six years. A smudge of rose chalk runs
along her hairline. We are standing
in a long customs line in Frankfurt. Finally we are
sitting down at our gate. Still hours before
our flight, it is mostly vacant. She chooses
to sit right next to me. I describe Portland
clouds, we talk about the ocean for
a long time. We discuss paneer and potatoes
with mustard seed and the trouble with finding
a good ghee. I say I can't make decent naan,
though I try with yogurt and flour. She half smiles
and looks at me sideways, "Even I have never made
a decent batch of naan." Scattershot of talk.

Forgiveness. Captive audience. Echo past
boundary crossings, this issue of being female.

Measure the worth of memory. I look in the face
of this stranger, her orange scarf lilting down
her shoulder, nod my head, tinker with gratitude and time,
lean into the space between two uncomfortable chairs
in an airport, gather up the inventory of ingredients
to store somewhere, to find again, for some reason,
while staring up at the smooth, white, curve
of an MRI tube, listening to gradient magnets
clang, thinking about curry, laying perfectly still.

LIFE EXPECTANCY, III

Do I believe in beautiful things?
The alphabet story reads
stay.
You are so perfect, a perfect number
divisible by infinity. It is not an ideal,
this maintenance of hope in the parts,
even if the sum is flawed.
A is for apple, cave paintings in Lascaux then
clay tablets from Uruk, we began writing top down,
sacks of grain, heads of cattle, outside then
inside, two parallel lines meant *friendship*
and in the meantime my language
for you is parachuting light streaking the
dark,
two parallel lines, you children,
lettering of enunciation–fix breakfast, pack lunches,
dinner fast it's late, everyone is hungry, everyone
is hungry, the dog is hungry, homework, baths,
proclamations, then past tense, you
grew up. Diction humming.

LIFE EXPECTANCY, IV

I return home after dinner
and a movie with neighbors,
click the door closed behind me
and burst into tears. You two,
worried, sit next to me
on the couch while I cry, hard.
You look at each other, I try
to explain: soon I will return home
to empty rooms, and tonight,
minus you, will be my
new life. It's not that I'm
not grateful for friends,
I am, but I'm more grateful
for you, I'm more grateful
for the fling me straight
into the flexing heart of
falling moments of motherhood
bathing me in intense and difficult
light for 18 years. Mom,
be happy, you say. Mom,
you're the most dramatic
person I know, the other
you says. Pluto's no longer
a planet, and someone
just told me figs are blossoms.
Would you understand
if I said in the country of my heart
figs are fruit, and all I know
is how to love you? All I know
how to do is love you.

SOUP

Chorus the exaggeration of this broad-shouldered minute.
This is trying to break me.
Split it in parts so the alto of yesterday's tumor
can nestle under the soprano of today's broken washing machine.
Sing louder louder, the tenor of forgetting,
the baritone of what could have been,
because the truth, the explanation, is silence,
is quiet nights of settling snow, my children
asleep, the fridge with two canning jars
of homemade minestrone from today
for tomorrow's dinner, already made,
already made. If you ask me how I am
this is what I will say: the soup for tomorrow's dinner
is already made.

FLIGHT PATTERNS

1.
Up along the Pacific
the highway winds at dusk,
rain statics

2.
Corners gathered,
bound with grass

3.
Snow outside Warsaw
I remember sheaths of ice
until the earth gave in
at its edge to the swallow
of the Baltic Sea

4.
Further north still,
the light dims and splits the day
down the middle of black and white,
and of how I tend to see things

5.
Spots of window light echo
from house to house
precise portraits,
hunched over a kitchen table,
stirring at a stove

6.
Corners gathered,
bound with grass

7.
I am making certain
to get home
on time

8.
Mikaelo sprays water straight up
calling the bees,
listening for the distant hum
of the oncoming swarm, waiting
for the din to evenly rise,
for the grey spot of sky to drift
to black overhead, to hover
then dive

9.
The sky is not maneuverable
by statistics

10.
The call and response
between physics and geography
is unwitnessable

11.
Yes, I love you

12.
Corners gathered, bound with grass,
We walk back out
through the brush, mosquitoes,

sweat our way to water

RED

"A ray of light was filtering through a joint in the lamp shaft."
—*Antoine de Saint-Exupéry*, pilot

We would wrap red paper around bulbs
and pile them in the corner of the hangar,
stockpiling emergency torches for when floodlights
were not enough. Because sometimes,
when night-landing at a port, fog lifts off the water,
and the sky lowers cloud-banks as if
with theater pulleys and moon fringe turns night
to ash but still doesn't clear the way to sight. And so
on descent sometimes, after a long flight,
one gives up on resplendent stars to chart a path home
one just gives up sometimes, you think you'll coast
into more and more black until the fuel and water
run out, until there are no more things
to think about, no more faces to remember,
no more cigarettes to shake for, jammed
alone in the cabin of a plane, and suddenly
a red dot appears below, sometimes several,
and there's always a second then, a moment
when I know I could pull on the throttle and
head back up into nowhere. And what nobody knows
is every time I almost do. I really almost do.
But then, I always push down instead and fall
past the clouds and arrive as expected.
My landings are always perfect.

FROM UP HERE

"We had been flying for three hours. A brightness that seemed to me a
glare spurted on the starboard side. I stared."
—*Antoine de Saint-Exupéry*, pilot

Fold the grocery list, here, I will tell you the sum of a day:
cat food, bread (wheat), apples, cheddar, Tunis, the Pyrenees—look!—
Sardinia—I flew in quietly, at a hundred seventy miles, coasting
between clouds, down, down. Might as well've been a glider,

but no. Ravel is drifting through the hangar as I climb out,
walk toward the boys, scotch. Now open the door. Time
for the daily walk. I wind my watch, the glass of its face is cracked
but it still keeps pilot time. I leash the dog. Today, the sky—grey and cold

like dawn in Cairo—makes me want to roll a smoke, haven't in 20 years,
we all smoked then, before take off, after landing, cigarettes and talk
around the card table of handwritten sky. I have forgotten my list.
Machine guns in Madrid, I could've outflown those artillery rounds

puncturing the sky like stars but we were on foot with militiamen,
I pressed against the stone wall, the sentry missed us and four hours later
I was dipping toast in coffee. Joints are swelling up again and I don't care
what they say, walking doesn't help, especially not with the dog pulling

on the leash. I tie him to the pole outside the market. Nineteen hours
was about my limit without water, I crashed in the Sahara and looking
for water I followed fennec tracks leading out of a burrow, winding
through shrubs. No one knows about fennecs around here. And sand

becomes theoretical and night a small tree to lay under and lick tears.
Orange juice. That wasn't on my list, but I know I'm out. I lean
on the cart, the aisles are narrow and sometimes I bump the stacks
of cereal, or the lines of cans. I have been in so much sky. Nowadays

I'm slow down the sidewalk, watching for cracks, a tangling of shadows
cast from overhead. But I sucked orange wedges in Marseille. I did.
I sat at that table outside and thought about the way camels kneel,
meshing legs like a zipper, and I thought about my broken altimeter

and wondered how long it would take to repair, I remember thinking that.
And now, I am waiting to pay, the lady in front is fishing in her purse
for coins, she tips the bag and shakes. Between the advertised specials
on the window I can see it is now drizzly, the dog is watching the door,

the grapes are ninety-nine cents a pound, and wind is invisible compensation.

"IT'S BETTER TO KNOW IN ADVANCE THAT WE ARE GOING TO FAIL."

(from *101 Experiments in the Philosophy of Everyday Life*)

I want to quote a letter:

> This is an older, radial engine biplane with top wing
> set forward off the bottom wing. His descent to land
> was at about a 45-degree angle. He wasn't just crabbing the plane,
> he was turning it pretty much sideways, reversing from left
> to right so the plane looked like a falling leaf.

I want to quote the sky:

> Progress can be summed up in noticing birds.

I want to quote my for-certain failures:

> I might fall asleep at the wrong time, the wrong time,
> do you hear me?, when I am supposed to be awake, shaking
> the trunk of a Japanese maple so leaves like feathers fall like rain.
> I surrender to solutions because willpower only takes me so far.

I want to quote water:

> There is a glass cup on the window ledge off the kitchen.
> It's been there since you were born. It collects what my hands
> can't hold, what I try to forgive while sleeping.

SMALL CRAFT THROUGH FOREIGN SKIES

The reed split and what happened was I kept blowing,
all cerulean-inking the air where sound met

NASA says:
>*[The speed of sound is actually the speed of transmission
of a small disturbance through a medium]*

I'm sorry I made us cry

>*[Disturbances are transmitted through a gas as a result
of collisions between the randomly moving molecules in the gas]*

Okay, so when I was standing in my kitchen saying I don't know,
now we know it was the randomly moving molecules

>*[Notice that the temperature must be specified
on an absolute scale (Kelvin or Rankine)]*

I forgot to do that

And I forgot how to do this, the now. Or I didn't want to remember

>*[The speed of sound in an ideal gas is independent of frequency,
but it weakly depends on frequency for all real physical situations]*

I think the real issue is I depend on you

>*[The dependence on the type of gas is included in the gas constant R,
which equals the universal gas constant divided by the molecular
weight of the gas, and the ratio of specific heats]*

Constancy, you say. Construct me a constant

>*[It is important to note that the sound speed in air is determined
by the air itself. It is not dependent upon the sound amplitude,
frequency or wavelength]*

Antoine was correct, you know. And all those
who fly small craft through foreign skies

> *[The speed of sound in the atmosphere is a constant
> that depends on the altitude, but an aircraft can move
> through the air at any desired speed]*

So we will be air

INDIVISIBLE

"Night and day, Lucas, who was the chief of the airport, would wind his gramophone; and Ravel's 'Bolero,' flung up here so far out of the path of life, would speak to us in a half-lost language, provoking an aimless melancholy which curiously resembled thirst."
—*Antoine de Saint-Exupéry*, pilot

Where ocean meets sky is a knife edge slicing earth in two perfect halves, and you are there and I am here, in half, reading a book about a French aviator who believed in twilight and charted his way through the Pyrenees by flying from star to star, and sometimes I tell one of our stories to a friend while standing in my kitchen, cleaning up from supper, washing dishes and drinking tea and wishing you could be ordinary, too, that these little wars of home could light a candle to Afghanistan or Timor or Liberia, that the landscape you know so well in Pakistan, mirrored the topography of me, a mingling light on the back of a mountain river in the Hindu Kush, the one you walk through, the one I imagine resembles you.

Looking down from the brim of land, Pacific rain
statics the forested hillside—could be rising off
the Burmese jungle or the promise of Bosnian hills,
wrapped delicately in green Tibetan silk,
corners gathered and bound with grass.

What I understand about geography is that you sometimes drive me nuts. I say that, you ask how. I deflect. You persist because that's what you do, persist, at being you, which in fact, sometimes drives me nuts, but most of the time I respect. Sometimes on windy days I watch trees. And the strongest branches always sway the farthest, batting about the air, holding on to nothing and everything at the same time. They always appear about to snap from the core. But they don't, they just make a lot of commotion conducting the storm. You do that, too. That doesn't drive me nuts. That I understand. What drives me nuts is that you call it flailing. And I call it orchestration. And upstairs, that afternoon, I didn't know how to say all that. So I started talking about Nicaragua instead. Or maybe it was Mongolia. As if the story of geography is a declaration. As if the story of a life could ever be told any way other than

through the sound of churning water on its way to some kind of eventual ocean,
rolling over and over like trust toward land.

Girl in yellow dress, cigarette, charcoal smudging
out the day's sky, bits of conversation
dropped into street grills, headlights against glass,
polenta and wine, somewhere warm bread
sunk with black olives, and earlier today mint rubbed
between fingers, a slope of clematis, rosemary, and vines,
the rusted leaves of a Japanese maple marking a birth,
roots holding onto the dirt, here, right here, where we are.

I could clip one leaf for each child, a tree slip for the marriage, reach down and
pull thick clumps of grass and clover for the years, gather dropped petals for
the rest, then throw fistfuls of this garden into the sky and watch the return of
all we believed we understood. Instead, I fold the New York Times' frontpage
in half, rip it down the score, give half to you, pocket mine, and while walking
home hold its corner and let go.

I seem to only be able to say part of what I mean,
and all the shoulds in the world line up like pennies.

APPLES OF SILK ROAD

I

The story goes that as the ancient Silk Road
wound through the mountains of Kazakhstan
monks and adventurers carrying porcelain,

ivory and bundles of tea passed through forests
filled with wild apple trees brushing the sky
at heights of 60 feet. Slips of wood

from these ancestral trees were grafted
in the second millennium by the hands
of Romans who used the technique to create

23 varieties of domesticated apples
that centuries later fill lunch boxes
and rest in ceramic bowls on counter tops

awaiting a shaft of morning light
to cut through the kitchen window
and arrange a perfect Cézanne.

There was a day when you would have walked
through that kitchen and grabbed that apple
on your way to work or the store;

but now your silk road winds through Central Asia,
following a pipeline corridor through villages
where parcels of farms are traded

to the village head man while geopolitical
alchemy simmers hope afloat in a tunnel
carved through the earth nudging a country's

internal politicking into celebration
that now, there is money to
marry off their sons and daughters.

II

At the height of the Silk Road transference
of 7th century philosophies, goats, and cinnamon,
travel skirted the ever shifting, city-swallowing

sands of the Taklimakan desert, its edges
contained by mountains and hidden grottos
holding the world's oldest books between frescoed walls.

Now its army of daily tornadoes and storms
unravel the lunar landscape with sudden flurries
of cone-shaped mortar collapsing the waves of sand

draped over oil reserves discovered here, too,
and for the last of the wild Bactrian camels, it's enough
to simply stand eyes closed against the wind and sun and wait.

III

A line segment of golden mean proportions
continually collapses onto itself, smaller over
larger, and this derelict thought winds

through the minarets, ditches, and flooded streets,
dependent on my will to haunt you, walking along
your new silk road. My finger follows the lines

of the Caspian region map, green for proposed
pipeline, blue for existing, and if those lines
curved or intersected, a star or spiral would frame

the topography of an arcing history,
the artifact of centuries of apples
dropping from trees despite tribal war lords

and multinationals, landlocks and rebel fighters,
you and I, centuries of debt
owed to the secrets of hidden things.

PIECES

We are mirrors of memory
and I am trying to love you
despite my definition

Do not think this is easy,
or that I am beyond humbling

Last night you both fell asleep early
and I watched wind, its evidence in
      the lift of fall leaves from trees,
      in the carrying of them across a backdrop of sky
      drifting down like
      the decay of piano notes
      when I give up on a song,
      tired of practicing, tired of hitting the wrong notes,

and yes, sometimes I want to give up,
not on you, but on happiness

That faint thud I hear,
it is the ghost limb of the engine turning in Makeni,
the rebel stronghold in Sierra Leone,
at the police check point,
the Ford Explorer
has to start,
they know, and I know,
I am not a doctor
on my way to the village
like my driver said,
and the longer we sit here,
the more patterns their fingers will tap
on their gun barrels,
it could even turn into a song
if we're not careful

BORDER CROSSING

There's a beat-up canopied pickup truck
crammed with men, stops a few miles out

from here hills underfoot
easier to hide, to slip through
around, under, get
to some other side

I can see you but you can't see me

Prayers said out into the canyon air down there
mingling with pinholes of dawn desert light

The deal with light is sometimes it's a consequence

And the problem with small spaces—pinholes, trucks—
there's more—light, room—on the other side

Light can't be trusted

Lose a day like a limb

Accumulation
divisible by riddles:

I cannot even save
my own children

So I get them a dog
And I wash strawberries for breakfast
And we talk about wars and borders
And this is our circumstance—

this is how sound travels

HOME

My daughter does not want to fall on the sidewalk.
    She is pointing the flashlight down, watching out
    for cracks. She is running up ahead, shouting warnings,
    "Here's one!" or "Look out for this curb!"
I am walking with my son.
He is humming a collar of song, there is rain, and we are waiting
for the first star of the night. It is a contest to see who sees
the first light first.

Flashlight directed up now, there is an oak on the parking strip,
its limbs buckling over, hunched branches like my back
on hard days. And when the beam meets the leaves pushed up
against the blackening sky, it is confidence.

I do not have enough time.

To tell you.

All the things.

My daughter has stopped running and is waving her flashlight,
shattering the dark, she could be conducting the sky.
I look up as I have abandoned the horizon, and I do see
the first star but I do not say anything. I want my son
to grow impatient with looking down on his own
and travel his eyes upward, extend his gaze like a branch.

I want to take the flashlight and stand against
the trunk of this oak on the parking strip, and shine it
straight up, and believe it will find a sleeping crow,
and when it does, the black wings will borrow the light, glisten.

TREATY

Remember the many little worlds
we each tried to start by banging stars together?

Your letters arrive like Darwin
slow descent to understanding

how light changes in a day,
that falling could mean landing.

I am not so interested
in your memories, or mine,

the way they and rain
sometimes fall sideways—

if I wanted to give up I would
but I am not so nimble.

A scrim of salt catches in the hair,
it is always windy at the coast

pushing sky to earth and that
is the secret I never told you,

that is why I always look west,
why I am envious of waves

so easily, obviously, crashing
because there is no way to land other than hard,

I want to make a treaty with the sky
like that chemist

who wanted to figure out air,
so he inhaled four quarts of carbon monoxide,

then carbonic acid, carbon dioxide,
nitrous oxide, through

a wooden mouth piece in 1799,
made lab notes.

He must have been a hell of a guy
to stand up to Aristotle

who believed air was pure, singular,
of one interpretation.

Last week when out looking for ruined things
I saw a coyote at the estuary,

he disappeared into the grass
but is still out there, so.

ADJACENT

3,741 miles and 7 hours time difference and I wake
to a message from you and a photo of the super moon
in the sky above my backyard. You write my dog
is running around in circles and sniffing things, you
made dinner, watched a movie, and are now waiting
for the moon. It only appears this big and this near
the horizon two times in a lifetime, though it's an illusion
NASA reports. Aristotle believed this moon illusion
was magnification from the earth's atmosphere, but
he was wrong, the atmosphere only affects the color.
And how is it, the moon appears bigger, but actually
in scientific factuality is 1.5% smaller when resting
near the horizon, than when dangling higher in the sky?
Cleomedes in 200 AD had a theory about apparent distance,
but another hypothesis maintains relative size perception
is dependent on retina and the object size in its environment,
how we see, thus how we interpret, the optical illusion,
as Ponzo and Emmert explained, so much science,
so many smart scientists over so many millennia looking
for fact, indisputable order, and explanation.

In Portland, like Iceland, the sky is often smothered
in gray clouds, there's no way to see the other side. But
you are patient with me. Science is not absolute, though
I want so badly for it to be so. But even Aristotle
was wrong sometimes. It's this perception business
that bothers me. How can something glow so brightly
against the black night sky, hang so low that it appears
to be dropping into the arms of the earth, how can
that be seen with actual eyes yet actually be imagined?
At the same time? You're asking me to trust the image,
the theoretical. I'm trying. The sky is above me,
I believe. The moon somewhere up there, too. You're
half a world away, and I'm bargaining with memory,
hinging the rest of my life on you and the sky between
us, splitting the distance between motives and coulds.

"YOU, HOWEVER, HAD TAKEN OFF IN THE HOPE OF FINDING A RIFT IN THE SKY."

—*Antoine de Saint-Exupéry*, pilot

Reconnaissance, colla voce
Mine. The kind beneath the creek
Down there in the mud, stuck between river stones

Lodged like sticks, step over
Beneath the creek, hide, seek.
Reconnaissance, colla voce

The water turns over, as though,
As though intonation can be believed
Down there in the mud, stuck between river stones

Murmur. Sediment in the cracks, holes
Pack mule's hooves clunk and splash to reach
Reconnaissance, colla voce

Crayfish, no, I told you—home
Periwinkle stuck to rock and reason
Down there in the mud, stuck between river stones

Greedy, in a world of such perfect isolation, no, open
Turn over the rock, clinging little invertebrate: speak.
Reconnaissance, colla voce
Down there in the mud, stuck between river stones

INVENTION

Invent the lives of others
Blue pajamas and the origin of the fall
I do not want the finch to hover

Before a finch can leave its mother
It must write its own song
And not invent the lives of others

As the day unzips each morning
And early hours collapse to a promise,
I do not want the finch to hover

And I will not see you as a concession
Or a placeholder for everything I miss
When I invent the lives of others

As if creating rain
To make the day gray and blameless
I do not want the finch to hover

Beating wings in stasis, dropping feathers
When instead its own call
Could invent the lives of others
I do not want the finch to hover

FUGUE

Pronunciation: \'fyüg\
Function: noun
Etymology: probably from Italian fuga flight, fugue, from Latin, flight, from fugere
Date: 1597
(In music) A musical form consisting of a theme repeated a fifth above
    or a fourth below its first statement, normally referred to as "voices."
(Psychogenic fugue) A dissociative disorder in which a person forgets who they are and leaves
    home to create a new life; during the fugue there is no memory of the former life.

    I. You are Still Here

It is E♭, the ring of the phone,
it is E♭ held
at two second intervals,
it is technically music,
the ID says payphone
you are slurring
you are standing somewhere
but won't tell me where,
so I substitute a street
it is anywhere,
and add a tree on the corner
and a red brick building up the block,
maybe a patch of pansies
in the parking strip,
and the occasional crow,
maybe it catches your eye
as you tell me it's getting bad now,
really bad, they're everywhere
as you tell me the police won't listen
or the FBI, you're trying
to make a connection
with the military,
suddenly you have to go,
I love you, I am mid sentence,
I love you the way leaves marry light,
they find their color
and then fall off.

II. On the Day I Realize You Are Never Getting Better

Repetition tricks the mind into thinking it understands mistakes,
memories, even the wrong words, if said enough times,
become easy to say. My shadow is not my multiplication
haunting the sidewalk, is not a wick re-lit over and over
until out of matches, so the walls can hold motion.
I stand in front of the candle on the table
and my shadowed limbs on the wall are of trees.

The parts resembling you are contained in the notes of me,
that is called evolution. Bach said
just hit the right key at the right time and the song plays itself.
Imitation of movement, if you hit the same note over and over,
tourniquet the song up a fifth, over and over, your voices become echoes,
each new voice a wing to hover in the chorale, beating back you.
How is it birds can fly so long and so far without stopping,
halfway across the earth, but whose earth, that
is what I want to know. And why in formation, why so ordered,
and to what home do they return, beautifully cluttering the sky,
chimney swifts, diving into soot? I'll make my own ash
by pinching the wick, I have blackened my fingers and now,
without light, I can no longer be your tree, though that is what I want.
Let me be your daughter.

Dusk gives up on the mirrors of light, no synonym of shadow
for reassurance, no standard crooned through the stereo,
Skylark, have you anything to say to me? A hint of history?
Tomorrow morning I will get up with the birds, I will wrap myself
in wool and go stand under the telephone wire and wait,
I will mimic smoke, open my mouth and breathe out,
over and over, to prove air, like all else,
can be seen on only the coldest days.

III. One stone takes you away, another brings you back
>   —Al-Shaykh, Hanan, *The Locust & the Bird*

"It's me."
I answer the phone and you land in the crater of my kitchen.
It is early, the light through the window like draped silk across the counter,
the air of coffee and toasted sourdough, quiet, the minutes of morning unfurling.

"It's me."
Your voice? The atom of sound hurling through space to vibrate against the tiny
bones in my ear? Where are you standing now? There is a horizon where you are,
it is my horizon, too. This is all I know.

"It's me."
I am slicing Asian pears when the kids shuffle into the kitchen, my right shoulder
is hunched up, balancing the phone to my ear. I lift my arms like wings as they each
take a side, wrap their arms around me, and I listen to you speak.

"It's me."
How is it there is more to know, yet fewer and fewer answers. This is not, not, what I
wanted to learn, about love, about maternal instincts. And I cannot find you
to tell you about the music, the kind when it is quiet, the kind since you have gone.

GLACIER DUST MAKES APPLE GRAFTS GROW

"The thing that made me so happy
    was I found this book at the library
with a picture of Monet's house in Giverny
    and it showed these two apple trees,
the Belle de Boskoop and the Reine de Reinette.
    And so today I brought my scion wood
to the farmer and I told him about those apple trees
    and he had the root stock for those, those
apple trees and so now I have Monet's apples
    on my porch. I hope they take.
I like espalier. They grow like a fence.
    I have the farmer graft because I don't like knives.
So now I'll plant them next to the Calville Blanc,
    And the Baldwin, and the Sommerfeld,
that's my favorite one, the Sommerfeld, though
    it's not an heirloom.

    "Did your dad bring those onion starts to you?
They're tiny ones. And sweet, like Walla Wallas.

"I'm very tired now.
    Glacier dust. I bought some glacier dust
at this place just over the Ross Island Bridge."
[What's that? I ask.]
"I don't know. Maybe it's dust from glaciers.
    It makes things grow. You should see my chard.
I'm very tired now."

[and then she hangs up. Just like that.

And I look up *Glacier Dust*
    it is trace minerals of glacial moraine
pulverized glaciers expanding, contracting,
    pieces of rock as big as continents

rubbing up against one another.
    Slips of wood with 3 or 4 buds
inserted in understock and we're back at Giverny.]

Belle de Boskoop: 1856, Netherlands,
    greenish yellow with dark red blush
Reine de Reinette: 1770, France,
    green with pink flush, sweetens in storage
Calville Blanc: 1598, France,
    yellow with light red flush, more vitamin C than an orange
Baldwin: 1784, Massachusetts,
    yellow flushed orange striped red, often a biennial bearer
Sommerfeld: 1984, California,
    a merging of *Fuji* and *Royal Gala*, her favorite

ENTOMOLOGY

*(As if turning on the light at 3 am
proves I'm awake*

        *As if things can be found
                by looking*

As if the truth can be changed)

You let the payphone dangle
after whispering:
*make them go away, make them
go away*

People without luck use payphones

Folding laundry is a waste of time

Disease is fruit flies hovering above ripe
yellow tomatoes on the kitchen counter
        They are not the dust of stars. Or you
        whispering into the phone,
        saying instead:

I'm here, I'm here, I'm here

BODEN CATALOGUE

Canvas Plimsolls, canvas outer, cotton canvas lining,
flexible man-made sole, toe to heel,
step in front of step until a hole is worn trying to find things
that disappear. It's possible to lose one's mind

Pintuck Tunic in "Bluebell Doodle Flower," our backyard
was speckled with bluebells. How do I measure
the distance between then and now, like my waist,
or length, the sizing must be right

Butterfly Slingbacks in "Honeydew." They are beautiful.
Impractical, like most essential things. If one can walk,
one can dance. It must be in the forgetting that I keep moving

Easy V-Neck in "Ice Blue Melange." Is there anything easy
about the place where two lines converge? Make a sharp point?
It is not a U, soft curves, a circle of arms

Essential Scoopneck, available in all colors. I am available in one.
Though, you have split yourself into many.
I am not sure which is real

Crinkle Jersey available in "Bright Green Daisy," except
daisies are white and yellow, sometimes pink, and if
a Gerber, can be shades of orange, red, this is what they are,
the reality of the situation, of botany, the leaves are green, yes,
and the stem, the part that holds up the color

Authentic Denim Mini, as in, Middle English *autentik*, from Anglo-French,
from Late Latin *authenticus*, from Greek *authentikos*, from *authentēs*
perpetrator, master, definition: worthy of belief as based on fact

Hotchpotch Top. They make up words in this catalogue.
Just like they make up colors. Just like you make up people
following you, creatures listening on the phone,
bugs in your light fixtures

Short Trench, in "Fennel" or "Almond." The kitchen, 30 years ago,
Christmas morning, smelling like Danish fennel rolls.
The origin of fenceposts, demarcation lines backwards,
my hand turns pages of beautiful people who are all, it seems,
you

Raw Edge Trim Top, Free shipping, free returns. When you
go out walking at 3 am
on what lip of earth are you teetering?
It must be quiet then, and dark. And cost something

Double Layer Twisted Scoop, page 90, in "Petrol Sun Spot."
I do not know where you are right now.
I do not know where you slept last night

Zigzag Belt in "Crocus." Mornings are louder in spring.
Like right now, it is early, dark,
the day is about to unzip, night going one way, light the other.
And there are birds. The bulbs you gave me
are pushing up the earth and unfolding

Statement Sunglasses. All right. I want to make a point.
This all happened too fast. I do not see what you see.
It's inside the lids of your eyes. My daughter asked,
just yesterday during our walk, why you
always wear sunglasses, even in the house.
Is it a disguise, she asks? Yes, I say

Corsica Kaftan. I do not know what that means,
but I like the way it sounds, and that's enough,
sometimes it's even a relief. This one works in "Blue 60s Swirl."
Those were your best years. I was a baby. You looked
like Audrey Hepburn. You wore sunglasses in the sun
because there was so much light, the kind seen,
the kind warm on the arm

AN OPEIDOSCOPE ILLUSTRATES SOUND WITH RAYS OF LIGHT,

by reflecting from a mirror and projecting
the vibratory motion of singing or speaking.

I am in Paris and wearing the grey and sage plaid coat
with big pockets and torn copper satin lining I found
at the flea market, les puces, and I am eating a still-warm
poppyseed roll from a Jewish bakery on rue des Rosiers,
I just turned on accidentally, it is early morning and it is
a long time ago. The acoustics of happiness are quiet.

I am walking toward the Miró sculpture garden,
the grey scrim of drizzle. I wipe my forehead with
my also wet hand. There is no logic to this, there is
no logic to anything that matters.

A fiberscope examines inaccessible areas.

I pass a concrete wall scrawled with obscenities
and I squint to see if the letters become inspired
if viewed through my cigarette smoke. A serimeter
tests the quality of silk. You push on my clavicle.
It is not silk, it hurts. Linguistic kinetics can be cruel.
Memory. With a topophone I could determine the direction
and distance of a fog horn. I can see but can't touch
fog, smoke, light. And I want to.

Selenoscopes view the moon.

Xathometers measure the color of sea or lake water.

There is a porch. I sit watching for a waiting morning
to leak through the singed night sky, a sky flawed like hope,
smelling of spice. These hours are untitled.

This was a long time ago. Last night was a long time ago.

Your eyes are blue.

And if I interpret this dream, there was kirsch after dinner
last night, and wild overripe cherries on your breath,
the breath holding words you don't speak out loud.

A goniometer measures the angles between faces.

Sometimes gratitude is in geometry. This is me saying thank you
for holding my hand while we sleep.

If I had a helioscope I could look at the sun.

BLINK

Blink
In the time it took to read that word
Cranial nerve 7
Ocular motor system
Corneal reflex
Reflex=no control
Reaction to light
A response to sound louder than 40-60 dB
The 5th cranial nerve initiates, sensing the stimulus
The 7th cranial nerve implements the motor response
Rapid rate of 0.1 second
In the blink of an eye
Dam breaks, heart stops, slip on ice, knock over the vase
"I love you" takes about the time of two blinks to say
Reaction to light
Long enough for everything to change
Short enough for everything to stay the same
If one has a parotid gland tumor, no say two parotid gland tumors,
    recurrent, amongst a swamp muck of scar tissue
    and encased in wound-around facial nerves,
    said tumor removal surgery risks the loss
    of the ability to blink. When this happens,
    little weights must be placed on the eyelids at night
Blink
The day the dam collapses is today
The day the dam collapses is every day, little deaths
    while flipping eggs, brushing hair out of
    the daughter's eyes, waiting at the mechanic's.
    Aquamarine, the sky might be aquamarine this day,
    opening up through the clouds, pieces through
    the kitchen window. Sky looks like water,
    water like sky, particularly if one squints.
    Or hangs upside down
Don't look down. The dam *will* break eventually,
    you can count on that. So don't look down
Disaster movies run out the reel, then the lights go up in the theater.

You can also count on that
The Poseidon Adventure; On the Beach; The War of the Worlds;
    Godzilla; Planet of the Apes
During the time it takes to watch one of these movies,
    the eyes blink 1,080 times
The river is bigger than the dam
The heart is bigger than the eye
In the time it took to read these words, cars crashed,
    breathing stopped, limbs broke, houses burned,
    guns were fired, someone was hit, someone was scared,
    depressed, angry, lost, drowned
Reaction to light
In the time it took to read these words, the sun
    came up somewhere on earth, somewhere else
    it sunk. A kid reached out his arms
    for his mom. Someone laughed, hugged,
    ran through a park, got a new job,
    graduated summa cum laude, ate lunch
    with a friend, walked their dog
Blink. Then quick, go. Keep your eyes open as long
as you can. It takes one-third of a second to
blink. That remaining two-thirds of a second,
that remaining 700 milliseconds—
That's all you've got

II.
And Other Sounds

RADIATION

It's mathematics. Angles, coefficients, line integrals. Algorithms. Formulas. Infinite numbers and inversions and rotations around an axis. Like last night, when walking down the hill toward home, you swung yourself around the signpost pole and twirled. It looked something like this:

$$p(r,\theta) = \int_{-\infty}^{\infty} \int_{-\infty}^{\infty} f(x,y)\delta(x\cos\theta + y\sin\theta - r)\,dx\,dy$$

You grabbed my arm, laughing at the dizziness. The autobiography of a day is told in the grey light of dusk. You tilted your head back and fixed your young eyes on the sky, walking that way for three straight blocks while I steered, pulling your arm if you veered too close to the parking strip, and warning of upcoming curbs. You said you were watching the day disappear, you didn't want to miss a thing.

Quantifying light. Rotation around an axis. Parallel beam geometry. I have a decision to make. I have a manila folder jammed with articles, abstracts, definitions, research study data, mathematical equations, charts, graphs, printouts from the Food and Drug Administration and the National Cancer Institute. They are smathered with highlighter pen markings and notes in the margins.

I work in photography. I arrange photos in a particular order to tell stories on walls, in books. I pull together exhibitions and write about such imagery, for cover jackets, for the interior essays. In one book about war and its aftermath, there is a picture of turkeys and geese in a foot-worn yard. In front of the house on a patch of grass is a table where three women sit on milk crates, breaking off chunks of bread, dipping in tins of soup. We are somewhere in eastern Europe. In another image, broken power lines reach down to earth like arms, the poles, straight like spines facing off with the sky. Lines run over faces, and across tilled, careful rows of soil; clothes wires divide the sky like a horizon, and serpents of pipes stretch out to the picture's edge.

So what, really, is relevant about images? In photography, there is aesthetic, and then there is just truth. Staring you straight in the eye: a burned-out building, ships moored by the circumstance of land, a spigot, a window, a door, chickenwire, clapboard, home, the inside of my son's head viewed from every angle. I have a decision to make.

There are patterns to how we survive. To how we fight wars, to how we contain our lives. Etched in the geography of memory is gesture. And it is within these gestures, and their repetition, that the stories are told. On whatever square of earth, we stand holding together all our parts: the threads of our history, the way our bodies merge with the landscape. We are pieces. We are broken. We are composites of the parts that stay hinged, stuck, wrapped in the arms of grey light, found.

I write about holding that light and the pictures of life it carries on its rays, placed on a piece of paper, and called a photograph. Alpha particles can be stopped with a sheet of paper. Beta particles, with a strip of aluminum foil.

...

Clarke's headaches are worse. His hearing is at an all-time low. There is 10% of a pearlescent orb still in his mastoid, the part they couldn't remove two and a half years ago. In the photograph the doctor took during the surgery, the mass is nestled in red, wedged in the bones. There is aesthetic, and then there is truth.

It all begins a long time ago. Clarke has just had his first CT scan. He is 18 months old. He reacts to the anesthesia. His torso is burning and fever spiking a degree a minute, while his extremities are ice cold and turning brownish blue. I sit in ER on top of a bed encircled by a plastic curtain while, for six hours, they try to stabilize my boy. After, they send us upstairs to the pediatric ward to stay overnight for observation. All the beds are taken by other sick children and scared parents. I curl around him on a mat on the floor. He sleeps. I listen to the children in our room breathe, I listen to the mother in the bed above me murmur to her daughter. I listen to the footsteps in the corridor.

Radiation. From sunlight. Radiation. Sunlight. Sky. The Rocky Mountains emit 40 millirems (mrem) per year. Three Mile Island, dose at plant site during the accident on March 28, 1979: 80 mrem. CT scans: 2,500 mrem.

It is 104 months past that night. Clarke's headaches are worse. I have one ally: an internationally-recognized otolaryngologist and neurological surgeon, also a professor and Associate Dean at one of the country's most prominent medical schools. I have fought with and dismissed over 30 doctors. He is the one willing to continue investigating. He orders another MRI, a new hearing evaluation. And another, 5th, CT scan. Then Clarke and I are to get on a plane and go see him. I cry rain because I have made a decision. I have to say no, to another doctor for another reason, again. One CT scan equals 312 X-rays. Clarke has had four CT scans, 1,248 X-rays. Clarke will have no more CT scans. And I am scared because it has been 10 years and I am rather out of doctors.

Clarke is rocking in his bed, holding his head, sobbing. It is night. And then it is morning. And it is the same.

CT stands for "computed tomography." A tomograph rotates around the axis of the patient, scanning, capturing cross-sectional images, pictures in parts, to create a tomogram, and the pieces become the whole. The etymology of tomography is derived from the Greek tomos, part, and graphein, to write. I write my way backwards. A pocket watch with a radium dial emits 6 mrem per year. Naturally-occurring radiation exposure is called "background" radiation—it comes from the earth, from water, cosmic rays from space, airborne dust and particulates in the atmosphere. The time period for equivalent dose from natural background radiation: 8 months per CT scan.

In 2008, researchers reported findings that 25,000 Japanese post-atomic bomb survivors were exposed to roughly the same amount of radiation of two CT scans.

One of those CT scan looks something like this:

$$p(r, \theta) = \int_{-\infty}^{\infty} \int_{-\infty}^{\infty} f(x,y)\delta(x\cos\theta + y\sin\theta - r)\, dx\, dy$$

An Austrian mathematician designed a mathematical basis for tomography called the Radon Transform—integral geometry, hyperplanes, equations, letters, numbers, symbols, mastoid, 10%, measure, image, logic, sky, logic, earth, pieces, logic, irrelevance.

Light.

Visible light is electromagnetic radiation. With it, I can see my son's face. Without it, I can see his shadow on the sidewalk under the streetlamp while he swings his body in a circle around the axis of the pole. A spiral scanner rotated around his head in one continuous motion in 2001, 2002, 2003, and 2007. Shooting in light, targeting X-ray sensors, in a perfect, algebraically-configured circle.

I let this happen.

...

At dusk, each evening of each day when you and I walk the dog up the hill and back again, the light, it is grey. It could be a photo.

RAMPS

"Mom, I need a ramp."

I'm washing up the dinner dishes. I have the flu. This morning I woke to a soaking couch and the living room hardwoods slick with water. It is spring in Portland. It is raining hard. My roof is apparently leaking. After teaching earlier in the day, I pick up the kids from their schools and we sit in yet another doctor's waiting room. It's half an hour past our appointment and we are still waiting. Clarke looks at me, "Mama, let's just go. They can't do anything any way." I look at him. "It's been nine years," he says. "It's not going to get any better."

"You don't know that," I say.

"Yes I do," he says.

I stand up. Soph puts down her magazine. We walk out. I tell him we are not giving up, that is not an option. Pain and hearing loss are at an all-time low. We have to boost his immunity, he has another infection. We have to deal with his resistance to antibiotics. I'm done with surgeons. Done. I call his acupuncturist, whom we haven't seen in two years. Needles and herbal concoctions are not Clarke's most favorite combination. I put his Chinese herbs in pudding, bake them in muffins, I buy a whole tub of frosting and mix them in that, spread them on graham crackers. Mix them in milkshakes. Nothing works, it's all disgusting. I tell Clarke I'll pay him to do this, a dollar a visit. He smiles and says okay.

So I am thinking about a lot of things, washing the dishes after dinner. Soph is in the tub, and Clarke still needs a ramp. I tell him to look at the house with ramp-maker eyes, I tell him I'll help when I finish. I finish cleaning the kitchen, put in another load of laundry and go to check the bucket in the living room. Across the floor Clarke has piled up CDs, books, tupperware. A cutting board is the main ramp, propped up with a book and plastic lids. The path leading to the ramp is a road of CD cases butted up against one another: Thelonious Monk, Sonny Rollins, Bill Evans, Paul Bley, Ani di Franco, Wilco, Smashing Pumpkins... Clarke has his remote control car poised on Tom Jobim, the first CD of the path, he pushes the lever and the car sails across the music, angles up the ramp, and plows straight into a stack of blocks topped with Steve Kuhn, Radiohead and The Arcade Fire CDs. They go flying. "Yes!" he shouts.

Tonight at dinner Soph calls a family meeting. She started something called the BLDCB, which stands for the Breakfast-Lunch-Dinner-Communication-Book and if anyone has something to talk about they write it in this little spiral notebook. Then we talk about it and end the discussion by going around the table and reading a poem, selected from a stack Soph keeps on the floor of the kitchen nook where we eat. This was all her deal, I had nothing to do with any of this. So tonight she presents an old empty tea canister in which she's placed folded up pieces of paper. She instructs us to close our eyes and draw three. It turns out they're new jobs for the week. I draw Harold (the guinea pig) feeding chores, setting the table, and Job Judge, which apparently is quality control...there is also the Clutter Helper (picking up around the house), food preparation (I had to modify that one a bit, considering no one but I knows how to use a knife or the gas stove...), and Ruby (the cat) and Clara (the other guinea pig) chores.

The poem book Sophie hands me tonight is one of Billy Collins's. I read a poem called Love. About a girl, a boy, a cello, and a train. If only it were that simple, I think. Or maybe it is, and I just don't get it. Clarke reads *Dog Love* from this kids' pet poems book. He takes every opportunity possible to remind me on my promise to get them a dog, finally, one year from this June. Soph chooses Paul Merchant, and his Greek translations of Yannis Ritsos, and straight-faced reads a piece that contains the words "A cigarette. And the moon on your breast." At which point she and Clarke double over in howling laughter at the word "breast," that lasts for seven minutes and results in spilled yogurt and rice on the floor.

We continue giggling throughout the rest of dinner. And in those moments I do not care about the roof. I do not care about the flu. I do not care about surgeons.

In our little family we play a game called, "I love you more than...," and depending on the mood, the stakes vary. One day it could be, "I love you more than green tea," at which point Soph will ask me, bagged or that expensive loose stuff you buy... again, my answer depends on my mood. Tonight while tucking them in, Clarke trumps my "I love you more than chocolate," with "I love you more than everything." Soph says she loves me more than the world.

In the world of our house, tonight after dinner, we noticed that the tiniest corn and tomato starts popped up out of the soil. Their little pots are on the kitchen table and the kids have been diligently spraying them with water. In maybe two weeks we'll transplant them outside. In the summer we like to sit on our back patio and eat from our garden.

My son does not believe his pain will ever go away. This is what he believes. And I can't change that. Can't seem to fix it. And every time I think about that, some piece of me somewhere cracks a little. He's right, nine years is a long time. I don't know what I believe in anymore. About medicine, about love, about war, about the weather. But what I do know, is that when my kid reads Greek poetry and erupts into laughter, or when the other one builds a ramp with my cutting board and CDs, that ramp extends straight to all the parts in me that hurt. And in those moments, quite literally nothing else matters except that exact map-pin point of geography where I'm standing, except that exacting light threaded through the needle to all the pieces of ourselves we sew together and patch over and over and over and over.

AN OPEIDEOSCOPE ILLUSTRATES SOUND WITH RAYS OF LIGHT, II

In the video from this afternoon, Clarke is holding Count Dooku in one hand, and Obi-Wan Kenobi in the other. He is making whistling and *whoosh whoosh pshoo pshoo* noises as he clicks their blue and red light sabers together. He has propped up my phone on his bed, placed it in video mode, kneeled down on the floor in front and the screen is filled with his face and the palm-sized action figures. His lips pucker with each sound effect, his hands move up and down and dart around as the Jedi and Sith battle. Clarke arcs his hand and Count Dooku nose-dives into the cushions. Obi-Wan does a little dance on the bed, and Clarke leans into the lens making his face larger than life, and whispers, "And he won…"

It is the night before Clarke's 10th birthday. The house smells of cinnamon and ginger. He always requests pumpkin pie for breakfast on his day. It cannot be store-bought. It must be made the night before so it has time to cool and set. Thus, it is 11 pm and I am writing while it is baking.

There are instruments for measuring or examining anything. Selenoscopes view the moon. Serimeters test the quality of silk. Topophones determine the direction and distance of a fog horn. Xanthometers measure the color of sea or lake water.

All summer Clarke has been making his films, as he calls them. There's one of me toasting a bagel. He follows the dog around the yard. A month ago he panned the phone around the interior of our car, my hands on the steering wheel, Sophie in the seat next to me with her headphones on, and then he turns it out the window as we left Wallowa County at the far eastern edge of the state, heading home from one of our summer road trips. The sky is blue and flawless like hope and he divides the frame in half at the horizon line and holds it there as we speed on toward the wheatfield plains outside Pendleton. Lucinda

Williams is on the car stereo and plays like the soundtrack to his piece. At the end of each little movie, he always turns the camera on himself, to grin, or to add some commentary. He's 10 and he has a signature, a look to what he makes.

He won't wear his hearing aid anymore, and I don't make him. If walking the dog, he'll move himself to my left so his right ear can pick up my words and we can talk. The rest of the time we make songs out of the word, "What?" Anything said enough times becomes some kind of truth.

Fifty-one and a half weeks out of the year I'm fine with this. A chromatoptometer measures the eyes' sensitivity to color and I have learned to lean into grey most of the time.

With a megameter I could determine longitude by observing stars. And sometimes I try. Most of the year, I try. Except for and always on the night of August 11, because I never sleep on this night. I am flooded with hospital memories. Divorce memories. Doctor waiting room memories. Setting the alarm every two hours all night every night for years to check on my son memories. Cleaning up the blood on crib sheets memories. Holding my sobbing son memories. Saying I don't know how to make his pain go away memories. On this night, I wait to take pie out of the oven and I sit on my porch in the dark and I feel like shit. And I let myself feel like shit. And I cry a year's worth of tears, and that's just the way it is.

I found a note Clarke wrote to himself today while waiting for me to finish teaching.
    Hi I'm Clarke and tomarrow is my birthday! I am excited. The sad thing is I can't wait. Here is my skedgewel...

And he outlines the day we have planned. He is asleep now, and he will wake early, and we will have pie.

MRI. Magnetic resonance imaging technology to obtain scans of the interior of the body. His last one was a year ago. It took 54 minutes. I was allowed in the room, to be with him, to hold his foot as it stuck out of the tube. With headphones he listened to a Magic Tree House book on CD I checked out from the library. He was told to not move, blink, sniff. I was told to not even shift weight from one foot to the other. The machine clanked and whirred. The techs and our doctor said it was unlikely he, at his age, would be able to remain that still for as long as was necessary to get the kinds and number of pictures needed. But he did. When they clicked off the machine and pulled him out, he sat up and one of the techs asked him how he did it. He said he pretended he was a Jedi knight.

There are instruments for examining anything. Except, it would seem, for looking accurately at my son's head and defining, resolving, the obelisk mother of pearl mass, 10% of which remains, embedded, enmeshed, stealing sound. The acoustics of happiness are quiet. Ideology, harmonics. The volume to promises, knobs twirling around and around, endless orbit to dial-in a waiting morning on the other side of a night sky that smells of spice, is bigger than I, black, quiet, and untitled.

SOUNDTRACK

Tonight my son and I have the evening to ourselves. We walk down to the corner Mexican restaurant for burritos, take a long loop home through the neighborhood, bake a batch of peanut butter cookies, play two rounds of cards while they bake, and with an hour left before bedtime he says what he'd like most is to sit on the couch together and listen to his favorite record, the wide-sweeping full orchestral Hans Zimmer/James Newton Howard instrumental soundtrack to the Dark Knight. He's never seen this movie but he loves Batman, and he loves scores, and this 74-minute cd addresses both.

There are clouds moving in as the light slips to other parts of the world. He leans against me and closes his eyes. His fingers draw pictures in the air as directed by the movement of the notes. When the violas hover his hands slow; as the horns move in, his fingers open and he twists his wrist back and forth. A cello lingers, his hands pause. "Did you hear that, mama?" I did. At least I think I did. It is difficult to know if I hear what he hears.

Piano notes string melody above a blanket of synthesizer on track three, ivory keys divided like days by black, and night brings shadow to the living room. I have not gotten up to turn on the light, the sky is dim and my son's body has become a twilight outline. I can still see his fingers tracing sound. He seems to know every movement, every transition, every fade, every build, of every track. I wonder how many times he has listened to this music.

I have learned over the years that he usually has the answers I do not. I break the quiet and softly ask what he thinks has been the lesson in all his medical issues, in his tumor, his chronic pain, his tinnitus. He keeps his eyes closed, takes awhile to answer, and then simply says, big and little. I ask him what he means. He says, "Little things don't matter, we have to save our energy for the big things that come along, like my head." He is eight.

I don't answer, we keep listening to the music. A moment later he says, "You know mama, it's okay. I sort of think all this has been okay." What do you mean, I ask. "Well," he says, "this is who I am. Kids at school, they think I'm cool cause doctors cut into my head, and it makes me different from everyone else. And even if the doctors could take out the parts they couldn't get last time, I would say no. I want it in there, cause it's me. And it's how I hear, even the tinnitus, even the headaches, it's me."

When he was four, he created a whole kingdom in his head that has since been built on and on, an elaborate story about bullfrogs bringing his headaches, and tiny bats only he could see sweeping in and taking them away. Giant 'thunderbeasts' cheered for the bullfrogs, and the chief chameleon would always determine which side had won each battle. Sometimes the bats couldn't help with his headaches because they had other work to do, such as making the oceans not flood. The bats would scrunch together their eyes really tightly and turn into the biggest bats in the world and hold back the ocean with their wings. He would start talking, usually while tucking him into bed, and I'd grab a notepad and pen and write while he told his stories.

A few days ago, a friend of mine and I had a discussion about what holds more truth, believing in faith, or in luck. Faith, he said, implies the work is done in spite of oneself, by our submission, our life is our life is our path. Surrender. Luck requires action, setting oneself up to receive luck should we be so lucky to have it grace our paths. Both require belief, yes; but luck requires a pragmatic alignment of forward steps taken, in spite of the path, in spite of the seeming course. To reconcile for oneself. To not surrender, under any circumstances. To believe in luck, is to squarely face the opposite truth, to know it very well may not appear. And to be okay with that, anyway, and to continue on with the life's work of finding oneself anyway.

At least at one point in each of our lives there is a dramatic pause, that point where nothing makes sense, or at least is not clear, and there is a rest in the score while we look around for the coda, some kind of permission or symbol or reason to gather our notes, to then throw them up to fly like dots of crows against a familiar sky, quietly and forward, toward bats and bullfrogs, toward descending nights, quiet, peanut butter cookies, neighborhood burrito joints, and eight year olds who already know who they are, who don't wince at needles, or at their mother's questions, or at the choice to believe in luck.

MAPMAKING

I am in Sandy, Oregon, at the base of Mt. Hood, and my tire is blown out. I'm waiting for the tow truck guy to help me change it, because I am inept and can't do this myself and Subaru offers this service for free. It was raining when I pulled over, but now it is snowing, and the sky, while darker, is laced and the thing about snow is it makes me look up. Rain, I just keep my head down. But snow drifts when it falls and stalls air and the moments it carries, and if I watch, I slow a bit, too, breathe for a second or two.

The guy's a little surly when he arrives. Grumpy. He's had trouble finding me, I'd left my phone in the car while standing outside, missed his calls. And while I did give exact coordinates to the dispatcher, they apparently didn't get relayed to him. He won't look me in the eye and lectures me about how he can't change a tire if he doesn't know where I am. Well, he's got a point. I apologize, thank him, apologize some more. In about 30 seconds he has my spare on, stands up, wipes his hands on his jeans.

"You don't have far to go, yeah?"

I tell him I actually have to somehow make it on this spare to Portland.

"You won't make it."

"I have to make it."

"Well, you won't. Tire'll blow out on the freeway. You're too far from home. These things overheat and aren't designed to go that far."

I shrug. We just look at each other for a couple seconds. We both know we're sort of remote and it's Sunday, the day after Christmas, and tire stores are all shut down.

"I'll just start driving and see what happens," I say.

He shakes his head.

Then his face suddenly just softens, he narrows his eyes and does a little half grin.

"Okay, then. Adventure. You know the back roads?"

"Nope."

"Okay, again. I'll make you a map. Don't go over 35 all the way home. You might be able to make it this way."

He climbs up in the cab of his truck and rips out paper from a yellow legal pad. He draws lines, and Xs, and labels roads and turns and roadmarks, like the John Deere tractor shop where I'll turn right, scratches his cell number on top.

"Call if you get lost, I'll set you straight," he says from his window as he pulls away.

It's mid-afternoon and the light is grey and dense and washes evenly over the sky, between trees. I've never been on these roads, up and down these hills. Tree farms quilt the landscape, a country market and brick tavern seem to appear every few miles. The occasional school. Farm houses set back from the road stream chimney smoke that mirrors the streaks of darkening impending rain held in the clouds. There is uninterrupted horizon out here, like at the coast when looking out across the ocean to some sort of other side, not meant to be seen, but wondered about, considered.

I haven't travelled this slowly for so many hours (and it does indeed take hours to get home at this pace) since the Sunday drives I think about for the first time in probably 30 years. My dad would come to the house and pick us up. My mom would sit in the front seat, and my sister and I would slide along the leather bench of the station wagon in the back. My mom always wanted to go out of the city, same kinds of rural roads as the ones I travelled today. She'd always ask my dad to drive really slowly so she could look at the horses and fence lines, wonder about the age of the farm houses. In the summer there would be roadside stands, and we'd stop and get corn, peaches.

I make it home. I pull into my driveway, sit there a moment, watch the picture of this piece of world out my windshield blur as the rain hits and stays. I send my mapmaker friend a message, telling him the tire held, thanking him for his map, which I kept on my lap the whole way. I walk up the steps to my house. It's warm inside, the kids and dog greet me with a clamor down the stairs.

I collect geography dictionaries and books. I love them. My favorite is from 1848, the title of which reads exactly: *Mitchell's Ancient Geography, designed for Academies, Schools, and Families, A System of Classical and Sacred Geography, Embellished with Engravings of Remarkable Events, Views of Ancient Cities, and Various Interesting Antique Remains, Together with an Ancient Atlas, Containing Maps Illustrating The Work.*

Kid you not.

Some guy named Henry Hickok carefully pencilled his name, and the date 1849, on the front page. I wonder who he was, why he had this book, if he ran his finger under the same lines I do. It's a funny book. There's a chapter called, "Greece, Italy, etc." (etc.??) and the first line in chapter 20, "Asia, etc." is, "The term Asia, as now understood, was not used by the inspired writers." Which made me laugh out loud the first time I read it. And a very large portion of the book is questions, "How many years have elapsed since the Creation? Since the Deluge? Since the building of the Tower of Babel? Where was Sicyon? Sidon?"

In *The Nature of Geography*, another of my favorite finds, published in 1939, the author writes, "It is the undemonstrated assumption that the landscape—the visible surface—is more fundamental to the total complex of an area than, say, the invisible climate, or the houses are more fundamental than the people who build them."

Or the map more significant than the way one stranger gets another to home—the visible and invisible kind, through dormant orchards, winding roads, memory, January sky.

FIGHT FOR YOUR RIGHT

Adam Yauch, aka MCA of the Beastie Boys, was on my mind all morning. As he often is. Usually accompanied by what has become almost a tick, to periodically throughout the day, every day, feel the right side of my head where my tumor was, where the new tumors are, as the surgeon instructed, in case bigger lumps appear, as they did the first time, when I absentmindedly felt the spot on my head while driving home from the beach the day after Dave's burial, and noticed a protrusion. The first surgery was successful, the facial nerves were spared, I can still blink, there was no cancer to spread. Yauch wasn't so lucky, by the time they reached his identical kind of tumor the cancer had spread, and he died, at my age, after battling the 2 in 100,000 people odds, and losing.

I have been shooting video somewhat incessantly since arriving in Iceland four days ago, 30-second held shots out my windows of this hat-off-my-head, grass and branch-bending storm that has not yielded, even for an hour, night or day for the past three. Since my surgery, and the recurrence of two tumors, I've been unable to look back, or ahead. The looking back part is probably good. The looking ahead part, well...abilities like hope, dream, plan—those are all held in the arms of the future, and I don't do that anymore. There are benefits to existing solely in the realm of the present—I feel everything. I notice more. Everything and everyone is right here, in front of me, and really quite honestly, nothing else. But sometimes the moments are too big to be contained in that particular moment, and sometimes they spill into context. And it's then I get into trouble.

I'm thinking if I shoot enough 30-second glimpses out my window, perhaps I can string them together with white space chunks in between, and perhaps I can form some kind of day, the kind of day that remembers, each frame leading to the next, from somewhere, to somewhere, and if I loop it, there will always be another frame to move into. I know this constructed metaphor can only take one so far. But this is what I can do right now in the belief department.

I'm writing a script to read over the video, and I delve into online research about parotid gland tumors, as I've done extensively since my own diagnosis, but I've stayed away from it for awhile, and now I remember why. It is scary. For some reason this morning I come across something I've never heard before in all my data scrutiny: for a tumor and cancer type with not a lot of known or quantifiable causes, hair dye is one that has been linked in 2-4% of the cases.

When one has a very rare tumor in the head, and survives a statistically risky surgery with no facial paralysis; when the relatively healthy, young father of one's children keels over for no reason anyone can find one random day while baking chocolate chip cookies; when one's son has a growth so rare in his head that the Stanford surgeon actually texts the mother the picture of it from her son's open head as she waits in the Stanford Medical Center garden—odds become tricky to negotiate. Statistics at once mean nothing, and everything. Every percentage matters, the tiniest. But the bigger ones, eh. It is nonsensical, I know. I worry not about breast cancer or a car crash, something I am more likely to be impacted by, but more about everything that shouldn't happen, but could. Because in my case, it has.

So when I read I can no longer dye my hair, that translates to I already have a super rare situation, I've got to take my breaks where I can find them. So, I superimpose my long auburn hair with solid gray hair, because I am indeed solid gray underneath that brunette wig of dye, and I am rushed ahead, at least aesthetically, 20 or 30 years. Which shouldn't matter, but regardless, I do have a good cry about it, and then have to pull myself together because I have a very important meeting in the sod house down the street.

Steindór Andersen is a rimur chanter, one of the only masters in the world. It's a complicated form with many rules, and Steindór makes it sound effortless. Syllables must be arranged in trochaic form with specific rules on the type of alliteration, rhyme schemes, meter, stresses and kennings. The vocal timbre must be a certain way, and the pitch raises semitones in specific places. The content is the ancient sagas and eddas, with short reiterated melody cycles, and there are even specifics on how to use the vibrato. My first night in Iceland I heard him perform, and sitting there in the echoing white-washed church the tones and reverberations of stories of my ancestors flooded the evening. There was nothing else.

Steindór is staying in the one-room sod-roof house from long ago around the corner from me. I knock on the door. The house smells of pipe smoke, and on the table are indeed two pipes, a carton of cigarettes, toothpicks, cds, and books. For two hours we talk. He tells me intricate details about internal rhyme schemes and alliteration and line breaks and stanzas. We talk about Thor and Odin. He shows me a velvet covered book with all the collected rimur melodies, passed down from generation to generation, collected and preserved, along with the song notation and lyric poems. They themselves are old, from before the 20th century, and the stories they tell are even older, mythological. But it is all about the things we fight for now—land, home, family, love, honor. We fight for these things, because they are all we have, and all we have ever had, and it has always been this way, and it has always been a fight, and in fights there are odds, and sometimes one wins, and sometimes they don't.

He tells me about performing at Coachella, and around the world with Sigur Rós, I ask him why the rimurs are important to preserve and to continue handing down to generations. Context, he says. To understand anything, you must understand the layers, you must look at the past and the present and the future, and that is why rimurs are so complicated, with so many rules, and so heavily constructed.

I try not to tear up sitting there in that tiny house. I ask him if he's still fishing, he's a fisherman when he's not one of the world's premiere rimur chanters! He says, no, he sold his boat because he keeps almost dying. Earlier this year he ate poisoned fish. Last year he had bypass surgery. He lights up a cigarette and offers me a beer as he pulls a six-pack from the fridge. He starts chuckling, realizing what he's doing in the moment he's tell me about his chest bone being pulled apart and his heart repaired. I raise my eyebrows and grin. He explains that coughing hurts him. And smoking helps him not cough, a fact I of all people, actually understand perfectly, because back in my smoking days, smoking made me feel at least like I was breathing better. Maybe it forced me to notice my breath more, to take it slower. I don't know. And maybe he's right. Like me, Yauch was incredibly healthy, a vegan and sought every form of treatment possible, including traveling to Tibet, and he didn't make it on this earth to witness his hall of fame induction.

I'm nodding my head in a way that must have indicated some deeper sort of understanding, and Steindór asks if I've had medical problems. I tell him about my head tumor surgery, and the recurrence of two more, and the unknowns, he offers me a beer again, as I'd declined the first time. I decline again, but what I really actually want is a cigarette. But that would be going way too far back into the past, and again, I don't seem to be able to do that. He asks my age, says I look too young for 47. I say, well, just wait til you see me next, I'll be all gray. And so it goes. Nobody's life seems to ever go the way intended or planned. The right angles of so many left turns result in the most peculiar and jaggedy of circles in the beginning, middle, and end of our life. It is luck, a sheer miracle, there is music, sky, birds, another day.

THE NIGHT STEVIE RAY DIED

I never never never in all my living days have understood how he got that sound from a crummy old tinny old Stratocaster, tones in anyone else's hands would be wheedle-thin, but that was Stevie Ray Vaughan. His signature was clear within a couple bars of one of his tunes spilling out the radio, the density of those notes pure unequivocal evidence that sometimes a conversation about bigger things occurs between musician and instrument. I had a music gig at the Laurelhurst Pub the night Stevie died. It was a duo with my husband, and I remember we were both too upset at the news of the helicopter crash that killed Stevie Ray to play our own tunes, so we just filled the place with Stevie songs, many of which I only knew the lyrics part-way through, but just let words find me and made up strings of things to sing about while Dave played the songs on his Gibson guitar, and so was born some weird hybrid hodgepodge of the memory of Stevie through his music and two young indie rockers at a bar in Portland, Oregon.

We did not sound like the stuff of legend, but if someone had told me that far into the future, some 21 years later, that night would be one stuck in my mind, resonating as some sort of validation for why we do the things we do…It was a random night, the bar fairly empty, a gig amidst many gigs Dave and I played throughout the 90s. I probably wore jeans and a t-shirt and my black boots. I had probably scrawled out the set list on the back of one of our posters while sitting in the passenger seat on the drive over. I can still see Dave plugging in the guitar, I my mic, we about to begin, looking at each other and saying, "This isn't going to work tonight."

Who knows what would have happened if the club had been jumping with fans or if it had been a Saturday night instead of a Monday? But with the gratitude that only hindsight delivers, I believe all the circumstances aligned to promote an evening that started out as any other and ended as a map pin in the geography of memory. We didn't break into one of our edgy folk tunes. Dave's fingers decided on a blues progression and for the rest of the night we riffed and wove our way through one Stevie tune after another, improvising off choruses, Dave's solos and my singing blurring recall with in-the-moment chord and word choices.

Like Stevie Ray, Dave was largely self-taught and never learned to read music. He had struggled with severe dyslexia his whole life, and credited this brain glitch with forcing him to find his own sound in his own way. And he did. The tunes we wrote together won national songwriting awards, charted across the country, and spilled out over five records, tours, and countless shows. And both Dave and Stevie died young. That's where the comparisons rest. Stevie Ray Vaughan's memorial statue is in Austin. There is no statue of Dave following his sudden death at age 44, but two decades following that night at the Laurelhurst, on the morning of the lowest tide of the year, our two kids dig a hole near Proposal Rock at Neskowin beach on the Oregon Coast and overturn the box we were given after Dave's cremation. Before covering the hole with sand they each scoop up a handful, their hands covered in ash like gloves, walk to the shoreline, bend down, and reach for the waves. After, we walk back to the rented beach house, all the cousins and aunts and uncles, Dave's brother and mom. We make waffles, the kids run around the yard. I sit on the deck and listen. There is a particular resonance to children's voices, their underdeveloped pitch. Gulls above squawk a peculiar fugue. The ocean fills every leftover soundspace. Sitting there, I remember Dave and I had to shout our vows on our wedding day to be heard over the waves as we stood on that very beach at Neskowin, giggling, "What?" Joking and cupping a hand to ear, "Eh? Can you say that again?"

But even the repetition of promises could not bind the threads of years like an unwinding spool uncoiling time spent like stitches and after twelve years together, the rings came off. I didn't sing for seven years after the divorce—not my songs, not improvised lyrics over the melodies of other songs. I could hardly even listen to the radio. And ten years later, on the night Dave died, my children's questions run through me not as words, not semantics, but as sounds, blurs of tones with a singular cadence, the language of hospital sounds, beeping machines and crying. The sound of Dave's mom sucking in her breath as she gasps over and over in a pattern, a rhythm, sitting in a chair in ER next to her son. I remember the music from Shrek 4 but not what happened in the movie. When we returned home from the hospital we crawled into my bed with my laptop. They had planned to watch the movie with their papa. So all night long we curled around each other in my bed and watched. I gave them bowls of cereal. I propped myself up in the middle, a child on either side.

I remember many dusks back in our music days, tired after a day of work, loading up the car with amps and cords, heading to another nosedive bar with no guarantee of even fifty bucks, wondering why we kept lugging ourselves and our gear out to play our songs over the din of clinking beer bottles and loud conversation. It took many years of accumulated age and life to realize we make experiences to make memories to call upon when needed. I couldn't have known then that sometimes, eventually, as elusive, unpredictable and abstract as memory can be, that sometimes these glimpses backward to the past are all that remain.

Sound rings off forever. There is no reconciliation point, even when it moves past our ability to hear. It's out there somewhere still, echoing. It's something to believe in, to know, even though it can't be touched or seen. Like faith. Music plays itself in how it's felt, in how the notes reverberate through the tiny bones in our ears, yes, but also throughout all the rest of us, a secular love rooted in the infinity of belief.

I confess to moments of quiet now. My son plays his father's guitar, dexterity in fingers that used to reach for me to pick him up. My daughter has a voice that is an anthology of divinity. I listen to them doodle around with notes while I'm making dinner or upstairs working. Without realizing, they're borrowing memory, too...mine, and transposing a kind of music that spills like light across a table. Sometimes I hear happiness. Sometimes I move through the song of our days like we moved through that night at the Laurelhurst, improvising, listening, being, remembering.

WHAT HAPPINESS LOOKS LIKE

It is Wednesday night. I am at an outer southeast Portland grade school, after hours, holding a poetry group for refugees and immigrants. I'm wrestling with the days, each of them this month, loss and sadness my clenched fists won't release and hope seems closer to the horizon line than to me. I almost don't go, I am too tired to teach, to figure out childcare for my two, to even go through my files and find lessons. And I don't know if anyone is going to show up. Sometimes the chairs are filled, sometimes not. I've been leading writing groups like this one for years now, off and on and on my own time, because I believe in stories and in the telling of them. Some days I think that's all I believe in.

Binh and Thomas and Lena are there. I've never met Binh or Thomas before. I write, *what happiness looks like* on the dry erase board because this is something I've been thinking about for a long time, and because I don't have any lessons prepared, and in hindsight, because perhaps I needed a little insight and didn't know where else to look.

We write for about 20 minutes. Then I ask if anyone wants to share their poem. Thomas is from Taiwan. He tells us happiness is only in moments of forgetting. He tells us that his wife died of Lou Gehrig's disease. He would wheel her chair to the park near their apartment and they would watch the children running, spinning on the merry go round, listen to them laughing, and they would forget she was dying, they would forget she was in a wheelchair, there was so much of the world at the park to absorb, in those moments it was bigger than them. In her final months when he couldn't take her that far, he'd wheel her out on their balcony and they could still see parts of the park, still hear the laughing and shrieking floating across the treetops.

Binh says happiness is in our dreams and hopes, but not necessarily in reality. He says it took him 32 years to finally successfully leave Vietnam. He tells of how difficult life was in Vietnam, difficult enough to spend an entire lifetime trying to leave. He has been in the United States two years. He says he was happier 32 years ago than now, when he had the dream of leaving, something to fight for, to believe in, some kind of bigger truth to be within. With a dream the past is leave-able, forgettable. Without a dream, we are where we are.

Perhaps standing here, on this soil, in this moment, is happiness, just the kind that is hard fought, moored in a harbor of memory and regret and loss, hidden.

Binh's daughter recently won an essay contest, and was flown to the US Air Force Academy in Colorado Springs for an awards ceremony. This prompts me to ask how many children Binh has. He says four. Then repeats four, three living. I ask what happened. He says one of his children died of a brain tumor 13 years ago. She was 10 years old. My son has had a mysterious mass in his head since birth, it has been a nine year, unresolved journey, and when I hear things like this my heart rattles about a bit in my chest.

He tells me of a doctor in St. Louis, an immigrant himself who at one time worked in the orchards in the German countryside, picking and carrying baskets full of fruit down swept dirt rows, until he became a doctor and landed in St. Louis. He is retired now, but throughout his medical practice he did what he could for third world children. Binh's daughter was flown to the US, where this doctor performed multiple surgeries. After one of the surgeries the child slipped into a coma and never woke up.

Binh and his wife named their youngest child after this doctor. Binh chuckles a bit and says, my Vietnamese baby with an American name. Binh tells me that this doctor has never recovered, has had an even more difficult time processing the loss than Binh himself.

This is not a happy story. None of these are happy stories. But for some reason on this night the continents and countries merge, Taiwan, Germany, Vietnam, America, and sitting in Portland on some plastic chair sized for a grade schooler, as the sky darkens outside on some random Wednesday night, our eyes well up, and for a moment it is quiet and still, and we're all looking down at the words we just wrote, thinking about the words we just told and heard. Binh is concerned about my son, I tell him he is all right, it's all okay, because in this moment, it sort of is.

Maybe this is what happiness looks like. Maybe it is all of this, in the forgetting, in the dreams, in the trying to save each other from tumors or tears, maybe happiness is sad, maybe we accept that, because we have to, because our stories, they are all the same, and maybe the comfort in that is bigger than us, as big as the horizon line leading to some distant land mass, and as small as a tire swing in a park with some kid hanging onto the chain, twirling, never to know the notes of her laughter reached an apartment balcony and wrote the kind of music that replays to memory in one man's mind for the entire rest of his life.

INVERSE CORRELATION

In an attempt to understand things we believe but cannot see or hear or touch, we assign them names, and request language ground the intangible. Whether recounting God's supposed word in the stories of the Bible, or the mythology of origin in the Prose Edda of the thirteenth century, we seem to need to create form—combinations of words we string together or stack or group in some way and then tell back and forth to one another or run our fingers or eyes over and somehow in that way these ideas, these manifestations of love and loss, of beginnings and endings, become real. The world is given, and then taken away, strong warriors fight to reclaim and hold their corner of earth, people are born, people die, and the Greeks, Norse, Native Americans—all of us everywhere and at every time in history tell these stories over and over and over, superimposing our own cultural references and characters and landscapes, but still, the events are largely the same. That this aspect of human nature is so consistent across time and culture reflects a need, or a habit, or a way of being that is necessary.

I am in northern Iceland, 913 miles and a softly arcing mapline away from my own Norwegian beginning stories, and I have a lot of questions, too, about things I don't understand, that can't be easily explained or ordered, in my mind anyway. I have plenty of names, but no way yet to compile them, or to at least attach a meaning I'm willing to accept. Words like *cardiac arrhthymia of unknown etiology with sudden cardiac death* from the medical examiner; *congenital cyst* in your son's mastoid, from the surgeon, and *inexplicable hearing loss, chronic pain, immune system deficiencies* from 15 years of other doctors...I don't like any of these words because I don't like their meanings and implications or that they are attached to people I love who, except for my son, are unable to say that word love back.

Anyone who knows me knows I hate irony. I don't appreciate it's appearance seemingly at times when I need it least, like when pulling together the packet of travel documents for our international trek. It's recommended I include my children's birth certificates stating I am their mother, as our last names are different, and also their father's death certificate in place of the written permission from a parent to take children out of the country. So this simple, benign-looking manila envelope holds all these pieces of paper with words that mean the beginnings and ends of life as I knew it.

Snorri Sturluson, compiler of the Icelandic Prose Edda, writes that one of the earth's characteristics is the seasons, a circle that never ends, blooming and blossoms followed by withering and dropping. It has always been this way, this inverse cyclical correlation, we live the metaphor of the exchanging hand-off of dark and the light literally every day as night and morning, it will always be this way. And when the land is scarred, opened or dug into, Sturluson continues, "grass grows over the soil that is closest to the surface." Grass to lie in, and look up at the sky. "People think of rocks and stones as comparable to the teeth and bones of living creatures. Thus they understand that the earth is alive and has a life of its own…It gives birth to all living things and claims ownership over all that dies. For this reason, they gave it a name and traced their origins to it." Over and over and over from today back to every yesterday, give it a name, plunge the flag in the soil.

Outside my five foot window the trees are ensnarled in wind and rain on the pane blurs the snow-topped mountains surrounding the valley I'm in. Did Sturluson, or Isaac Newton for that matter, really get what they were saying? Whether framed as seasons or laws of physics, for every force there is the opposite force? And if people die, or the body revolts with illness, or if an entire village, like the one I'm in right now, loses its industry, is the inverse correlation to that what remains?

So, what remains, is the question. There are patterns to how our lives are lived, and to how they're lost. Last night I ran through the rain up the hill to the white church to listen to two violinists, a violist, a cellist, a keyboardist, and a rimur chanter fill the echoing nave with songs in an Icelandic tradition dating back to the fourteenth century. There are places on earth where some things remain, and are remembered, and brought forward through song. Repetition, recurring themes, patterns of alliteration and rhyme, the telling and re-telling of stories in the Edda all mark the rimur tradition. I sat there, on a literal level not understanding a single Icelandic word. But I did understand story, beauty, history, human experience, music translating life, and somehow that recontextualization transcended everything else.

And now it is late afternoon the next day, there has indeed been another rise and fall of day and night, and over the thrashing wind against the window I hear my children upstairs. Sophie is singing, and stops every few minutes to talk to Clarke who is drawing. There are moments, like last night in the church, like standing at the top of the mountain rising above our village yesterday overlooking the fjord into the foreverness of the ocean extending beyond into everywhere, like right now listening to my kids, where I can see the validity of this theory of inverse correlation. Though Newton may disagree, it seems to not be an exact science, there is no way to measure loss against gain. But in those moments of pure alignment of goodness, it doesn't seem to matter.

In one section of the Edda, Thor is dead from the serpent, and the wolf swallowed Odin, but Vidar will kill the wolf, leveraging his foot on the wolf's lower jaw, to allow his hands to grasp the upper jaw. Sturluson writes, "He wears on that foot the shoe that has been assembled through the ages by collecting the extra pieces that people cut away from the toes and heels when fashioning their shoes. Thus, those who want to help the Aesir should throw these extra pieces away."

I imagine it's a matter of balance. The weight of accumulation can skew cause and effect, offset the momentum necessary for happiness. The wind that is hurling itself against my window now will be replaced by stillness, there will be quiet.

III.
What Remains

SITTING IN A HUT WITH A RIMUR CHANTER

Back in the old days,
they wanted to hear
the stories intoned,

not acted out, not sung,
not merely told, and then
a prayer would follow,

and then sleep. Night
after night this habit
repeated until it became

a pattern, or pattern
until it became a habit.
Never breaking fully

into song, but never plain-
speaking, somewhere
inbetween the way

I tell you ordinary things
about the spent day in my
ordinary voice, and the way

birds release a new day,
before anything has happened
except the miracle of waking

up again—the tumor didn't
kill me tonight. Patterns imply
a before and a to come,

a rolling over again, again,
is it a habit to stay alive?
Patterns break. Somewhere

in between the beginning
and the breaking is
no wishes, no inevitable,

just the sound of stories
with end rhymes and internal
rhymes, the same sounds

repeating so that in any
language the ear notices
the vowels and consonants

surviving the nothing
hushed-tone days, and singing,
despite themselves, all

the way to all we've got.

VIBRATO

"Iceland's Herring Adventure (1867-1968): Herring is one of this century's principal shapers of Icelanders' destinies. Without herring it is questionable whether the modern society that now exists in Iceland could ever have developed."
—*Icelandic Historical Atlas*, Vol.3, p.40

> Context is the only way
> to know something, he says,
> and demonstrates by
> chanting a rimur verse,
> holding out the last word
> thickly wrapped in timbre,
> vibrato holding on and
> letting go of the note
> at the same time.

MIGRATION, II

"With the Herring Museum – Siglufjörður's wounds from the disappearance of the herring in 1968 have been healed."
   —*Ólafur Ragnar Grímsson*, President of Iceland,
   speaking at the inauguration of the Boathouse, July 24, 2004

>   Migratory patterns shifted,
>   and the herring all just went away,
>   swam to the east side of the island
>   and never returned. But a man
>   decided to tell the story of how the fish
>   came and fed the village for decades,
>   and then all just went away,
>   and along with them, many of the people,
>   too, but some remained, and
>   continued living. Everything changed, he tells me,
>   everything—the piers at the harbor rotted,
>   population declined (he gestures with his hands,
>   making a downward spiral). But he wanted
>   a museum for a story about what people
>   can do in a small place, about identity,
>   and what remains because things remain,
>   especially memory, he says, to continue
>   writing the story that began generations
>   ago, and hold it in this building, instead
>   of tearing it down, and pretending
>   the truth of a place ever leaves.

MIGRATION, III

My home was our home and then
it all just went away, but if
I believe the truth of a place
never leaves, then something
remains, and if I believe in
the interdependence of context
then that story is part of this story,
and whether it is happy or sad
is in the telling. I have been trying
so hard to forget. But I cannot retell
something I don't remember, I cannot
replace the rotten two by fours if I
do not see them, and I cannot see them
if I will not look. How fragile,
wood like lace, where carpenter ants
and termites burrowed tunneling
through the beams, how fragile, wood
like lace, barely there, except still there.

THE WALTZ OF SIGLUFJÖRÐUR

The Waltz of Siglufjörður is earth-toned oils
on canvas, center frame a man sitting on a herring barrel
holding a squeezebox, villagers encircling, the harbor

and horizon in the background. It is a balanced
and composed scene. It is always light here
this time of year near the Arctic Circle,

even with the shades drawn, the pitch of day
remains ever-morning and I can't sleep and can't let go
of the wish for dark. Patterns are hard to break.

But then again, so is the time signature of a song,
1-2-3, 1-2-3, beginning-middle-end, past-present-future.
When one breaks into spontaneous laughter (repetitive

breath expiration), the average sustained duration
is 3.7 seconds. All 3 chest wall compartments engage.
It takes 2-3 breaths upon laughter cessation to

resume normal breathing patterns. This is science,
it is balanced and composed. But I laugh out loud
to test the theory, and find the breakdown of an exhale

is in the pattern of a waltz, my laughter is rhythmically
a waltz. The souvenir of all our years apart is a waltz
and we will dance and laugh, and I will learn how

not to be bothered by the light.

Emil Thoroddsen, 1898-1944, studied art, as well as music, in Copenhagen. He was best known as a composer and pianist, playwright, critic and translator. Thoroddsen's best known paintings include *Siglufjarðarvalsinn (e. The Waltz of Siglufjörður)* from 1922.

GLOSSARY

The search party embarked at dawn
to look again for the lost hiker,
wandering or fallen somewhere in
the mountains. Several hours in,
unclear if it was a tern or a yell or
the wind ribboning the trees, someone
thought they heard a sound. So
they followed the sound, until it became
a word, and then many words like
breadcrumbs scattered across the terrain.

*

The painting still exists of people dancing
on the dock, ship masts top left,
mountain peaks spanning across, hands
on waists, feet turning and turning, heads
nestled on shoulders. Imagine what words
got caught under the breath—it was a good
harvest, or the fish ran plentifully that year.

*

What remains is forgetting and remembering
trading places like inhales and exhales,
good years, bad years, lost, found,
I forget to nail the words "thank you" to
each morning, to each person who loves
me, who forgives me. Yesterday I find
a folder with notes from ten, twelve years
ago, scraps of paper, and pieces of brown
paper lunch sacks, where I'd scribbled things
said by my tiny kids in ordinary days:
Clarke asks if we can make thunder soup.
Mama, I'm going to run like laughter.
Mama, there goes a flock of old people.

Mama, there's a glasshopper.
Sophie tells me a story about a little boy
whose Chinese lanterns all blew away from
his backyard, so he made new ones out of
leaves and blossoms and kisses and wishes
and they grew to be lanterns the size
of houses and filled his backyard and then
floated up into the sky to light the rest
of the world. Mama, she says, life,
you can change it. You can do it by
the simplest things. Accidentally, maybe.

EYES LIKE MINE

When my ancestors wrote, it was in memory
of the dead and on stones. There would be no reason
to carve rock to discuss the sky, one need only
to look up. No reason to remark about grass fields
or waves hitting land, one need only to look down
or across. With nowhere to look, nothing to touch,
even the Vikings knew it is only words that remain.
Odin speaks a spell, he can carve and color the runes
to return the dead to life. He proves it on himself,
dangling from a tree, he will walk and talk again.*
Seventeen centuries later from when the first runic
inscriptions date, I write to remember, daily and with
velocity to catch up to forgetting, in a house atop soil
where perhaps a few hundred years ago, someone
with eyes like mine, carried a body, lit a fire, drank water.

---

* Stanza 157 of the Hávamál poem in the Poetic Edda.

KEEPER OF BELLS

> The shaping gods drove ashore
> the ship of the keeper of bells;
> —*Njal's Saga*, chapter 102, section 10

Echo past recognition into this hello, I'm still here
in this afternoon of forgetting when it was all easy,
there was a time when it was easy, we just didn't
know it. We didn't know time runs out. We didn't know
history is only made when remembered and we certainly
didn't know how to be happy. But we thought we did.
I'm watching glacier water spill over a cliff at the
largest waterfall in Europe. I walked down the path
from the parking lot, expecting to hear thunderous
crashing of water down the 150 foot drop to the
canyon river flowing out to the Greenland Sea.
But there is no sound except birds until topping
the hill and facing the waterfall directly. Which makes
no sense. The weight of melted mountain
throwing itself down and across earth in a route carved
from the eruption of the volcano sitting under it,
and there is no sound until you look at it, see it fall.

ROCK-PAPER-SCISSORS

This morning I ran up the path
into the mountains, turning to look back
I could see the small cemetery at
the west edge of town, it's large white cross
marking the square plot of land sacred.
It was supposed to rain, but bright sunlight
soldered the sky to the ridge instead and
it was then I thought of you, still sleeping
in the upstairs room, all of you transparent,
the infant-preschooler-teen blurred together,
soft, quiet, shuttered from the world, soon
to waken, sit up in bed, and look out

the window. There's a story about us,
maybe about every mother-daughter,
it goes rock-paper-scissors. Palms fisted
at my side, shaking. Then flat hands cupping
your beautiful face. I like to think of
scissors cutting your hair, trimming
the curls but I know it doesn't mean that.
You are about to leave, make your own
home, maybe somewhere in the mountains,
maybe California. Maybe the birds
will crowd your sky like they did mine
this morning, filling it with song, causing
me to look up and notice the seam between
earth and sky, reminding me of you.

MONOLOGUE, I

*One smile may transform darkness to dawn
like a single drop all the nectar in a bowl.
Warmth can switch at one word of scorn.
Proceed with care in the presence of a soul.
So often a heart hid a string that broke
at a bitter retort made for no sake.
How much life regrets a single look
which never will be taken back.*

—*Einar Benediktsson* (1854-1940), Starkadour's Monologues

You owe me nothing,
and I certainly

do not owe you my regret

strung like lights
over window frames,

along ceiling seams, around

my neck—whichever surface
I can find. I wanted

to do this better. The sky

is perfect, the horizon,
birds, but not I. I wanted

to mother you with perfection,

to tune each day
so all the sounds

pinging off my edges would align,

you would not notice
the dissonance, you

would hear only music.

MONOLOGUE, II

When they
removed the mass
in your head,
we assumed
your hearing
would improve.
When it didn't,
how much life regrets a single fact,
which never
will be changed,
your sister and I
began speaking
a little louder.
You turn your head
to your good ear,
listen to half the world,
only nothing
is missing
because it has always
been this way for you,
whole in its parts.
I must remember this.

MONOLOGUE, III

"People did not know
where his kingdom was.
Because of this,
they believed he ruled
over all things on earth
and in the sky, in
the heavens and
the heavenly bodies,
and in the sea
and the weather.
In order to recount
these beliefs and
to fix them to memory,
they gave their own names
to all things…" * and so
I named you Clarke, and
so you named your tinnitus
the island of Tanarina
and headaches thunderbeasts
and giant bullfrogs and Sunji
who was actually
a baby elephant,
and nothing was fixed
and nothing changed
but we told stories,
and it became
that most days
I realized the stories
made more sense
than the medical reports,
and the "I don't knows"
from the doctors, and that
was the darkness
and the dawn,
the earth and the sky,
the myth and the legend

that became the truth,
the nectar in the bowl,
the only nectar in the bowl
was those nights,
laying on your bed,
listening to you
tell me
your stories,
"Mayor Chameleon
gives everyone maps,
they're magic and just poof!
into the air
the kingdom animals
fall down like parachutes,"
you said, and I pictured
a sky filled
with parachuting creatures
drifting closer and closer,
to a waiting field
at the crest
of a hill
in the middle of nowhere
but still somewhere.

---

*From the Prologue, 1. In the Beginning, *The Prose Edda*, Snorri Sturluson

APOSTROPHE

What has remained: the sound
of oceans and geographic coordinates
of mountains and fjords carved
by glaciers, and 18 million years later,
in my middle age, I sit here as if I matter,
an apostrophe to generations of
Norwegians and Danes I never met
and never will. Answer me: I keep asking.
Correlate the statistics of family, scatter plot
what's left, it needs to make sense, to graph
a picture, ah, I see it now, it all makes sense now,
the lines connect and arc, dip and bow, like
the lines a conductor draws in the air
to reveal the music, to cue the cellist, the oboe.
Except it doesn't, there is no sense, there is no
picture to frame and hang on a wall, the architecture
of want is need. What has remained: answer me:
I keep asking. The sound of oceans could be music
to certain ears. The latitude and longitude
of immigration crisscross could be a net, your
father sailed to South America from a small town
in Germany. Your Danish mother ended up in Ohio.
During the war your husband worked the docks
in Chehalis, looping anchor rode to the piling
or cleat hitch in a bowline knot to secure the ships,
and he thought about sonatas and seven-part
rondos he used to play and compose,
and then drank and was mean. So
you left him once the children grew and finally
met your love, and then he died, and you
stayed alone all the rest of your decades,
and called your granddaughters and rescued us
and baked filbert cookies and reminded
me to pray. What has remained: answer me:
I keep asking. Before you died, you asked me

to wash you, so I rubbed your sagging skin
with a warm towel, rubbed lotion
on your hands and neck, changed your
bedding. What is left I need to want less.

STATISTICS

Statistically speaking she lived
21 years longer than she should have.
My children have memories
of her reading to them, singing
them Jesus songs while holding
them on her lap, wrapping them,
even as big kids, in that pink
flannel blanket. My daughter asks:
Why are you so upset, you had her 46 years,
she says, peering at my face, *I only
had daddy 12 years.*

I should
                             be happy.

LUMPFISH

Lumpsuckers are not attractive fish,
to be sure, and some say their meat,
after curing and boiling in water,
is too strong. They can barely swim,
out of proportion roundish bodies
with lines of wart-like protrusions and
too-small mouths trawl near the ocean floor,
surviving on stationary or slow-moving prey
they can actually overtake. But the name,
Greek in origin, means circle wing, round
pectoral fins fluttering about as they hover
around rock and mud substrate.

At the base of the mountains
at the edge of the fjord is a farmhouse
where a kettle full of lumpsuckers is boiling
on the stove, expanding the air in every room
to a soft sweetness, and friends gather for hours
and tell about themselves, and sing old songs,
and eat fish traditionally eaten for generations,
the ugly, acquired-taste fish whose name
means circle wing, and outside the house
it is raining, the arctic terns dive and rise,
a plane has just been shot down in a country
a few degrees east, there is war it seems
wherever the compass arrow points.

Circle wing. The fish is soft and rich with oil
and needs only to be gently nudged off
the spindly bones. What remains? My children
sit on the couch, plates on their laps,
quietly listening to the music, the talking,
and for right now, for a few hours, they have
all they need. The house is warm, the people good,
the meal and traditions and history shared.
I would rather remember moments like these.

I would prefer to wonder at how stories
of the sagas remain to be chanted
in a rimur 800 years later, to eat fish
caught in an ancient ocean and prepared
and cooked the way people have been
preparing and cooking this fish for centuries.

I have already forgotten the sound of your voice.
For a moment our children, Dave,
have what they need. They are surrounded
by what has remained. I would rather remember that.

ANCESTRY

There seems
to be nothing
to forgive.

Migratory patterns
shifted. There is
an explanation,

and no promise
is ever
truly kept,

not by the earth,
not by you.
Climate change

or death
provide the easy
answers;

the reasons
are more
complicated,

hinging on acceptance,
and that maneuvers
my heart away

from you.
And so
I won't.

The herring
headed east.
I'm up north,

relying on genetics
to reveal the way
across, like air,

moving through
what it can,
around what it must.

The Norse people
conquered every
piece of land

their feet touched.
Every piece of land
they touched

became
a new home.
Somewhere inside

my platelets remember
how to do this,
remember how to clot,

how to find home.

ABOUT THE AUTHOR

Kirsten Rian's poetry and prose have appeared in numerous publications. She has been awarded artist fellowships, grants, and international residencies, leading creative writing workshops both domestically, as well as internationally in locations like post-war Sierra Leone and refugee relocation centers in Finland, and with human trafficking survivors, using creative writing as a tool for literacy, community, and peacebuilding. She has been a volunteer language facilitator for non-native speakers for 20 years. Her anthology of Sierra Leonean poets and their accounts of the civil war, *Kalashnikov in the Sun*, was published upon her return from a fellowship in West Africa. She is also a photography curator and multi-disciplinary artist.

kirstenrian.com

For other titles available from redbat books, please visit:
www.redbatbooks.com

Also available through Ingram, Amazon.com,
Barnesandnoble.com, Powells.com and by special order
through your local bookstore.

www.ingramcontent.com/pod-product-compliance
Lightning Source LLC
Chambersburg PA
CBHW020939090426
42736CB00010B/1195